The
Flight of the Earls

A Drama

by
Christopher Humble

A Samuel French Acting Edition

SAMUEL
FRENCH
FOUNDED 1830

New York Hollywood London Toronto

SAMUELFRENCH.COM

ISBN 978-0-573-61946-5   Printed in U.S.A.   #810

THE CHARACTERS

The Earl Family

Michael — around 35 years old

Brigitte — Michael's wife, 30 years old

Ian — Michael's brother, around 30 years old

Keith — Michael's brother, 25 years old

Kate — an older woman, the mother of the three Earl men

The Strain Family

Timothy — Brigitte Earl's brother, 18 years old, he has a stammer

Claire — Brigitte's and Timothy's sister, in her twenties

The entire action takes place in the Earl family home in County Tyrone. September, 1971.

Act I

Scene 1
late afternoon

Scene 2
an hour later

Scene 3
half an hour later (night)

Act II

Scene 1
immediately following

Scene 2
early the next morning

Scene 3
an hour later

THE FLIGHT OF THE EARLS

ACT I

Scene 1

The house lights dim to a blackout A voice fades in slowly in the darkness until it is completely audible It is a recorded voice of a man making a news report During the broadcast the lights come up slowly and we discover the Earl family's living room/dining room area The room is plainly furnished, without any luxury There is a settee and one large, comfortable armchair next to the fireplace, stage left Near the armchair is a very large, old radio in a wood cabinet Just in front of the settee is a small coffee table Downstage of the fireplace is a small desk. The dining area is downstage right A door from the dining area leads offstage to the kitchen. There is another door upstage of the kitchen door which leads to the upstairs of the house We can just notice the first few steps of the stairway Between the two doors there is a breakfront Some whiskey bottles and glasses are placed on it, along with the family's good china and a telephone next to the whiskey An entrance door to the house is situated upstage just left of center (the UL door) There is a small window just next to the

door and, under the window, a wooden bench with several
sets of shoes underneath There is a wooden coat rack on the
wall just next to the window The time is summer, 1971
Late afternoon TIMOTHY sits stiffly on the settee He is lis-
tening to a small pocket radio We soon realize that the speech
we are hearing emanates from his radio During the broad-
cast the volume drops until we hear only the radio which
TIMOTHY is holding IAN enters through the UL door
IAN crosses quickly to take away his radio He turns it
off

IAN. Oh, Timothy Timothy Timothy You're looking
pale, lad You've got yourself in a mess, isn't it? You've not
had beatings here before but likely this time'll have to be
the first. You amaze me, lad It's not every family would
even take in an idiot boy the likes of you.

TIMOTHY. I've not done nothing, Ian

IAN. Oh Timothy You have You have indeed

TIMOTHY. I've not done nothing bad I'm no   id
idiot boy, Ian. Don't be calling me no idiot.

(MICHAEL enters quickly through the UL door He crosses the
room to TIMOTHY)

MICHAEL Timothy Strain, how many times is it I've
told you not to go into that garage?

TIMOTHY I . . I ... 'Twas.

MICHAEL Answer me, boy. Or it's the back of my hand
you'll be feeling

TIMOTHY.   only for a tool, Michael My bike is broke.
The wheel

MICHAEL. How many times is it? Answer me!

TIMOTHY. M ... many times, Michael But ... you wasn't here and   I ..

MICHAEL. Aye. You needed a tool for your bike.

IAN And who is it going to show you how to use a tool, Timothy? And you a dunce itself who couldn't...

MICHAEL Shut up!

TIMOTHY. I'm not a dunce. I know myself, Michael, how to fix my bike, for Keith showed me many times and .. and said I was no dunce if I could   . do it.

MICHAEL It's Keith you're always talking about, Timothy. And him in jail the year already and not coming home soon What about me and Ian, Timothy? We've tried to be your friends, haven't we? *(TIMOTHY nods)* And what about the rules, Timothy? That's our barn It's me and Ian fixed it up as a garage Haven't we got a right to make some rules in our own garage? Must you be beat to learn the rules? I'd not want to do that.

TIMOTHY You .. wasn't here. I knew I'd .. find the tools in the garage

MICHAEL And what about Michael's telling you to stay away from that garage? You could get hurt in there There's lorries jacked up that could fall. There's electrics that can shock There's petrol and combustibles that could blow you to pieces.

IAN. It's no place for a boy that's not got all his senses.

MICHAEL *(Shoots IAN an angry look.)* Timothy, I don't want you getting hurt.

TIMOTHY You wasn't   here. .

IAN. Tools are in the garage, Timothy. You weren't

near those tools a'tall You went right past the tools to the back to have a look, didn't you? Never thought we'd be coming home so soon

TIMOTHY I won't again *(He stands and tries to get his radio from IAN IAN doesn't give it to him)* I p   promise I . won't. . *(He crosses upstage and starts to exit through UL door)*

IAN *(He stops TIMOTHY from leaving and pulls him over to a chair He sits him down.)* Now Timothy I want you to tell us what it is you discovered in the garage *(He squeezes TIMOTHY around the neck. TIMOTHY grimaces)* What did you see that you never knew was there?

MICHAEL Take your hands off, Ian!

IAN. *(as he moves away from TIMOTHY)* I'm only trying to get the boy to talk. Go on, Timothy Tell Michael where you were when I found you That's what I want him to know

TIMOTHY I .. I was in the small room .. under the garage At the back. Underneath the garage

IAN. Michael Earl, I told you we should keep that garage locked Jesus Christ!

TIMOTHY It isn't nothing new, Michael. That room . is nothing new

MICHAEL. How is it you know how new it is?

TIMOTHY I know 'twas last October you started to build it.

MICHAEL. How do you know it was last October?

TIMOTHY I know I saw, didn't I?

MICHAEL What is it you saw?

TIMOTHY When I was sweeping   and . and cleaning up in front of the garage I saw the l . lorries coming in I saw each time a lorry was fixed, there'd be a small load o'dirt in the back when it left. 'Twas empty coming in. I.. I knew that... the dirt was coming from inside the garage. I knew you was digging out a hole... a room... and. and p ... putting the dirt in the lorries.

MICHAEL. Have you told anybody about that room, Timothy? The underground room.

IAN. *(He laughs)* The secret room!

TIMOTHY. I ... have not, Michael...

MICHAEL. Timothy .

TIMOTHY. God's truth I have not, Michael.

MICHAEL. Not even Brigitte, Timothy? You'd not keep anything from your sister.

TIMOTHY I never spoke a word of that room to nobody.

MICHAEL. Brigitte's your favorite in all the world. You've told Brigitte surely

TIMOTHY. I haven't.

MICHAEL Why is it you haven't?

TIMOTHY. I'm no talker. I'm no id ... idiot says everything. I know what ... what to say. I know . you been keeping it secret.

MICHAEL. How is it you know that?

TIMOTHY. The room's hid. Under the garage I knew you was .. b ... building it .. c ... careful and secret.

MICHAEL. Timothy, do you know what it is we do there?

TIMOTHY I don't.

IAN The room's not empty, lad. Tell us what you saw there.

TIMOTHY. I saw nothing. It's dark. That room is .. d ... dark.

MICHAEL. *(He crouches down next to TIMOTHY at his knee.)*
One day he's seeing empty lorries going out with a pile of
dirt. Scotland Yard right here in County Tyrone! And
another day he's looking at a room full of all kinds of
things and seeing nothing a'tall. C'mon, Timothy. Which
is it?

TIMOTHY. It's dark down there. I only saw ... at the
front. I only saw a ... workbench. And ... parts ... and electric wires. Nothing else, Michael. I ... swear it. It's dark
down there.

MICHAEL. What is it you think that small room is
for?

TIMOTHY. I don't know. For electric repairs? For radios
in the cars?

IAN. Tell us what else was in that room?

TIMOTHY I can't think of nothing else. It's the truth.

MICHAEL. It'll be worse for you if you're lying to me.

TIMOTHY. There's no word of a lie in it, Michael. It's the
truth. I swear . the truth.

MICHAEL. For you see, Timothy... there's many a good
reason why we've got to keep it a secret. You see ... we're
afraid .. for if anyone would find out we're fixing electrics
we'd be in jail.

IAN. Aye. For there's a union, Timothy, for electrical
mechanics. And we don't belong. We're just trying to
make some extra money.

MICHAEL. Aye You know   what with Keith in the kip
and us paying bribes to try and get him out. And with you
and Brigitte and me planning to go to America. You can
see how it is we need the money, Timothy Brigitte can't
know for she'd not approve of it. And you'd not want me

and Ian to be in jail, too, would you?

TIMOTHY *(He pauses, looks up at IAN and then back to MICHAEL)* I wouldn't.

MICHAEL Then you'll promise, Timothy Not a word to anybody?

TIMOTHY Not a word I swear, Michael

MICHAEL Good boy Now, go and fix your bike

TIMOTHY *(He stands and starts to exit)* I'm sorry, Michael for going inside I won't again I promise

MICHAEL Timothy Don't forget your radio *(TIMO-THY crosses to get his radio from IAN IAN tosses it into the air and TIMOTHY just barely catches it He begins to exit again)* And be quick with that bike You'll be going to Stephen Boyd's for some things we need

TIMOTHY I'll hurry *(TIMOTHY exits through the UL door IAN crosses to the upstage window to watch TIMOTHY disappear from sight)*

IAN He knows

MICHAEL I'm not sure There's a joke A year's careful building of that room And being caught by a simple boy and them keeping their sharp eyes on the two of us the long day and night Damn! Why now? Why'd the boy have to see it today?

IAN Michael, he knows and he's just waiting to tell somebody You know he must've had a look around

MICHAEL Everything's still covered And it is dark. He didn't have a light on, did he?

IAN He could've shut it before I got there.

MICHAEL He said he didn't look I don't know if he's smart enough to lie about it

IAN All these months of planning One dunce of a

boy will ruin it all I've told you that boy's a damned curse...

MICHAEL. And I'm tired of hearing that. Try to remember how many times it is he's carried things all over Belfast for you Who else could you get to carry your little boxes? The face of an angel on that "curse" of a boy. He's promised not to say anything.

IAN. Michael, that's a chance we can't take

MICHAEL. We'll send him over to Stephen's. At least 'til we're finished with Faulkner

IAN. Michael, they're pulling in men without charges. He might not even make it to Stephen Boyd's We'll not have the Prime Minister in our laps again One word from that boy and they'll be on top of us.

MICHAEL. He'll get to Stephen's

IAN. Michael! We've got people depending on us. Just one word from him

MICHAEL They'd not take in the likes of him for questioning. They'd only stop him long enough to see he's slow

IAN. They would question him, Michael They know about Keith. You know they suspect the whole family Whatever that boy has seen he'll tell them

MICHAEL. And what can we do about it now? I can't tie him up, can I?

IAN Michael, think of tomorrow! Think of all we've spent.

MICHAEL. We'll send him to Stephen's 'til tomorrow night. Then I'll talk to Brigitte about having him go to Claire's

IAN. It's not enough, Michael! We've got so much

planned We've got to be sure he never talks.

MICHAEL. What is it you're saying? I know what it is you're suggesting and I don't want to hear it. He'd not break his word to me.

IAN. Not on purpose he wouldn't. Michael, they took in sixteen men at Dungannon yesterday. And they're torturing some. You know that boy wouldn't stand it for a moment.

MICHAEL I'm sending him to Stephen's.

IAN What if he's picked up after that? There's still a danger

MICHAEL You'll not be talking about doing something that has nothing to do ..

(KATE's voice is heard from offstage The men continue talking over her lines which we barely hear from the distance)

KATE *(heard in the distance)* Timothy Strain. Timothy! What are you doing sitting there on the dirty ground? You'll ruin those trousers. Timothy! Are you listening to me? Timothy!

IAN *(overlapping KATE's distant voice)* Michael Someone's coming *(He crosses over to look out the window)* It's Mother

MICHAEL. *(overlapping KATE's distant voice)* No more about Timothy.

IAN Aye For the moment.

MICHAEL We're finished on this subject, brother Keep your mind on the plans and let me .

(KATE enters through the UL door She is carrying a bag of groceries

and a dress box)

IAN. Hello Mother.

KATE. Just what I needed, Ian. Those strong arms. Take this into the kitchen. *(KATE hands the bag to IAN She removes her hat and coat. IAN starts to exit to the kitchen, but he stops when he hears her mention TIMOTHY)* Blessed saints, that boy's gone deaf. Pays me no mind Ruining his best trousers. Wait'll Brigitte sees him with grease stains on the rump. She'll be in a fit.

MICHAEL. Hello Mother. *(KATE offers her cheek, which MICHAEL kisses)*

KATE. You're in for a treat, boys It's a fine meal for the Earls tonight. A celebration. I thought you'd be in the garage

IAN. Aye. We should be out there, working. Instead of being here talking about it. *(He exits to the kitchen.)*

KATE. *(to IAN as he exits)* Your favorite thing to discuss And I hope you've said it all. It's no time to be discussing it this evening. *(to MICHAEL)* Claire's coming and I want us to be having a grand time when she gets here. I'll just have a small sip, Michael, as long as your pouring. *(MICHAEL crosses the room to the breakfront, stage right, and pours his mother a glass of whiskey)* You know how fond I am of Claire. I only wish she'd come for a visit more often. I like a travelled woman. You can learn things, you know. You can hear about the world past Dungannon I'm not sure it's there, mind you, never having seen it. But I've heard stories *(MICHAEL hands KATE a glass of whiskey She sits on the bench to put on her house shoes)* Oh Michael! You should've seen the crowds at the market. My aching feet! I gave Mr

Curley a cold eye you can be sure when he said he hadn't saved me a nice bird He was teasing Well and isn't he always? *(IAN returns from the kitchen)* Flirting with me, that's what it is you know, plain and simple. And me not a widow these ten years Oh! *(KATE stands and takes her dress box)* And wait'll you see, Michael, Ian, what I've got!

IAN Is it my good whiskey you're drinking, Mother?

KATE You mean "is it your good mother drinking your cheap whiskey?" When was it you brought a good whiskey into this house? If I weren't parched near to death from shopping for the likes of you I wouldn't reduce myself to having a sip a'tall *(She crosses to the settee and sets the box on the coffee table)* It's the dress I told you about, Michael. I had it put away They've got them in all the stores too and it cost me just eight pounds It's a bargain at twice that I showed it to Mrs Dougherty before I bought it. She told me no Christian woman would wear this color And her the dumpiest old thing this side of County Armagh! *(She pulls the dress out of the box)* What do you think?

MICHAEL It's lovely

IAN It's a non-Christian blue surely, Mother

KATE And you the devil too I wanted something nice For Claire Well, I'll be in to start supper Where's Brigitte? Probably already at the cooker Brigitte!

MICHAEL. Not home yet

IAN Are you coming, Michael? I'll be out to the garage to finish working Billy McIntyre's lorry

KATE Don't be running off the two of you! The day's over Billy McIntyre's lorry's been waiting the week. Another day'll serve him right for trying to keep the old thing on the roads Sit quiet there why don't you Ian, and have a whiskey to get you in the mood *(She crosses to pour the boys a whiskey)* I want us to be having a grand time for Claire's visit. The way we used to Can you remember that? Claire and Brigitte coming over and having a fine time with my three boys Well, two of 'em anyway Come day, go day, and into the night we'd sit and laugh The third one always the stuffy one Always off to his work and never a laugh on his long face.

IAN Not much to be laughing at if you're listening to what's happening in this place. There's men being put in jail for no reason

KATE And here's your old mother thinking only of new dresses and laughing at the whole world I'll not apologize for taking a free day now and then, Ian A few good times is called for. Give us a smile for this once, won't you? I've already met with one long sad face on my way in the house What's wrong with Timothy? Hardly said hello. Sat there staring at his bicycle as though he'd seen the saints coming for him It's not like him

MICHAEL Well, we had   we had some words

KATE What's he done?

IAN He doesn't listen to no one That's what. He does what he wants and doesn't answer to no one

KATE It's you had the words with him, Ian, isn't it? Why is it you can't be more patient? The both of you When Keith was here it was him you were picking on Now Timothy's getting all the trouble Shame on the both of you

IAN He doesn't listen

KATE He listens well enough to those that talk civil to

him. It's hard on him, Ian, coming into this house. Trying hard to be one of the Earl boys, them not wanting a stuttering boy. He doesn't listen to you, Ian Earl. It's because you treat him like he's not wanted here. He's got feelings too. I'll have to go and try to get him smiling before Claire gets here I want her to think that he's treated well by the Earl family. *(She exits through the UL door)*

IAN. Will he be telling Mother now? You can never be sure. How long is this going to go on, Michael? We've got to get rid of Timothy

MICHAEL. Stop it! I'll not listen to that. Your own brother-in-law You've gone mad.

IAN. There could be an accident.

MICHAEL There won't be an accident!

IAN. Michael, we've got to do it. You've got to realize what it is we'll lose, brother Years of planning Maybe our lives. Michael, the British Army spent the day searching through the houses in Lower Falls They'll be here too. That "secret room" will be no secret, that boy knowing what he knows.

MICHAEL No!

IAN. And think of all the filthy Orangemen who'd rejoice at the finding of the likes of you and me with a room full of surprises Think how they'd love to take your property The last of the Earl property sold at auction A fine day that would be.

MICHAEL. We can't, Ian. Our own family.

IAN He's not our own! You're the brave one gambling with several lives I've a stake in this too You're the one who married that girl

MICHAEL. Don't you dare to call my wife that girl again.

You'd do well to find yourself a girl half as good

IAN Well don't you be asking me to accept her retarded brother into my family What would Dad think? He was willing to die for Ireland Do you think he'd get this close and be stopped by a simple-headed boy?

MICHAEL I think he might've tried to find another way

IAN We have tried And it's not enough! Think of our ancestors watching all three of the Earl boys falling on our faces. Keith Stupid enough to get caught with a nail bomb on him Now us Being done in by a retarded boy Dad'd be proud, wouldn't he? It'd be the flight of the earls all over again Four hundred years and still running

MICHAEL We can't, Ian We just.

IAN Remember, it won't be just you that falls down They'll have all of us if they have you We don't know if the lad's had a look at your ledger book down in your secret room

MICHAEL He won't say anything He'll

IAN It's not easy to hold your tongue under torture You might not even be able to do it The British have been torturing them, Michael Joseph Clark said they used electrics on him

MICHAEL I'll not do it, Ian! He's everything to Brigitte

IAN Then we're dead surely And our plans for tomorrow are dead too The Prime Minister will go on killing Catholic men in all the Six Counties His rich Protestant family can go right on making shirts in that lovely factory in Cookstown Right here in County Ty-

rone Still owned and run by a dirty Protestant pig The
great Earl of Tyrone himself is turning in his grave. It's a
proud moment for the family again. My own brother's
gone soft. Maybe it's time to take a rest, Michael. It's not
right, risking our lives for an idiot boy who won't live to be
thirty

MICHAEL. Brigitte loves Timothy

IAN She loves you more. What will she do without
you? I suppose she'd go on to America and take up with
one of her cousin's Irish-American friends A young
woman the likes of Brigitte   she'd have no cause to be
faithful to a husband who's in the kip for life. Or dead,
more likely

MICHAEL Shut up

IAN. And don't you see? It'd be Timothy's life for the
cause. It'd give meaning to his life If he's killed we'd be
forever free of suspicion. That, and Brigitte and Claire
working so much with the ladies' peace group, will keep
us clearer than any men in Derry Tomorrow, Michael
Think of Brian Faulkner! It would destroy Brigitte if you
were taken from her But, I'm thinking she might recover
in the arms of another man One of those handsome
Irish-Americans.. *(MICHAEL turns around quickly and
punches IAN in the jaw IAN falls backward onto the floor The two
men look at each other for a moment MICHAEL tries to help IAN
to his feet but IAN pulls away, crosses to the UL door and starts
to exit)*

MICHAEL Ian God forgive us *(IAN turns slowly and
comes back into the room)*

IAN We've got no choice, Michael They'll interrogate
him surely It would be our deaths then For Ireland,

Michael. It's worth all our lives. It's what Dad believed in. Think of him.

MICHAEL. Aye. I'm thinking of him. Do you think Dad ever had to...

IAN. Where'll we send him?

MICHAEL. Send him?

IAN. We may as well make good use of him. It ought to seem like a likely place. It'll work as a diversion for tomorrow while we're at the factory.

MICHAEL. Aye. You decide. *(He crosses to sit.)*

IAN. How about Clifton? Antrim Road. The bus station for Coleraine and Portstewart. There's British on duty there too. We'll have Timothy wait for the ten o'clock bus. Only the bomb will go off a little sooner. And you'll stay here at the house, for Brigitte and Mother will be here. And Claire is coming! And isn't that the perfect alibi! The living, breathing leader of the Northern Ireland ladies' peace group taking tea with the Earl family! I never thought I'd see the day I'd be glad to have Claire Strain coming to my house. I'll go to MacAleery's in Pomeroy for a few pints with the lads. There'll be a large group for my alibi. If we're asked why Timothy was at Antrim Road we'll say he was on his way to Stephen Boyd's. I'll call Stephen to back us up.

MICHAEL. But you'll not tell him of the plan.

IAN. No. I'll make it seem real. That Timothy's to pick up some parts from him.

(The telephone rings)

IAN. *(Crosses to answer it.)* That's real enough, for we've

sent him many a time Make a list, Michael   for Timothy
to carry Some things we would need for the garage *(into
telephone)* Hello   it's Ian Who's this?   Aye You're sure?
(He covers the receiver with his hand and turns to MICHAEL)
Danniel Jesus Christ *(back to the telephone)* When? Aye We
don't have it, man Where do you think we   We'll try! I
know we need him! Aye Haverhill I don't know when.
I'll try   Jesus Christ, I'll try! *(He slams down the receiver)*
They've taken seven men in and Danny O'Farrell is
one of 'em

MICHAEL Damn! I can't get near that factory without
him Damn!

IAN You can get him out They're saying for a "certain
amount" they'll let him go

MICHAEL How much?

IAN Two hundred pounds

MICHAEL. Christ! We haven't got it! Two hundred
pounds! I've got to have Danny! Nobody knows that place
like him

IAN How much do we have in the shop?

MICHAEL Maybe eighty Christ!

IAN You could get it from Brigitte

MICHAEL I don't know if she's got that much

IAN Tell her it's for Keith She's always given money
for him A good deal more than £120

MICHAEL Aye But never all at once

IAN You could tell her it's the final payment Keith's
freedom is worth everything to her, Michael That's her
ticket to America With you We can say we've had a call
They're saying he'll get out if this bribe is paid We won't
get another chance like this at Faulkner, Michael

*(TIMOTHY and KATE can just be heard as they come toward the
house They are laughing)*

MICHAEL   She might not have the money...
IAN.   You've got to try, Michael. If we don't have Danny
we don't get.

(KATE and TIMOTHY enter through the UL door)

KATE   We've just fixed Timothy's bike
TIMOTHY   I . I . fixed my bike Keith showed me
KATE   Aye Aye It's true I was just in the way
MICHAEL.   That's good, Timothy. Maybe we'll soon
have Keith with us again. You'd like that, wouldn't
you?
KATE   What about Keith? What's happened?
MICHAEL   We've had a phone call We have to send
money
KATE   Michael Earl Don't be a fool.
MICHAEL   It's got to be done, Mother You know
there's others has had to do it.
KATE   You're being a fool You don't even know if the
money's getting to Keith a'tall. Sending your hard-earned
money for nothing
IAN   And it is our hard-earned money, Mother, isn't it?
Let's not start this up again.
KATE   I'm telling you not to do it and   I know how
much weight my opinion carries in this house Keith'll be
laughing at all of us here when he finds out what we've
paid for him. And how it didn't help him a'tall. *(She crosses
to IAN)* It's your hard-earned money is it?

IAN   We've not asked you for any, Mother *(KATE exits up the stairs TIMOTHY stands and begins to follow her)*

MICHAEL   Timothy *(TIMOTHY stops and faces MICHAEL MICHAEL brings him back into the room)* You can help get Keith out sooner You'd like that, wouldn't you?

TIMOTHY   I wouldn't I like the bed to myself.

MICHAEL   But he'd teach you things Like before It'd make Brigitte happy too You'll help, won't you? We want you to deliver another bribe, Timothy, on your way to Stephen's For Keith We've had word   and   we want to deliver some money Maybe he'll get out sooner Will you help us again? Like you did before

TIMOTHY   Aye

MICHAEL   Good boy You'll be going to the bus station in Antrim Road You know the way You'll take your bike

IAN   You're to sit on the waiting benches Like you do when you're on your way to Stephen's in Limavady Put the package of money under the bench and you stay there until ten Exactly at ten you'll leave the package It will be picked up after you've gone You'll get on the bus for Stephen's Do you understand?

TIMOTHY   I do

IAN   Repeat it for me, Timothy What it is you'll

TIMOTHY   I've heard you I   I I don't need to say it a. again I'm no   idiot I'm taking money at ten to be picked up   like before I'm no idiot, Ian

IAN   *(He begins to exit through the UL door)* You wait here for a few minutes We'll get the package ready And Michael's going to finish making a list of things he needs at

Stephen's We'll call you from the garage Are you coming, Michael?

MICHAEL Timothy Have you got your radio?

TIMOTHY It's here

MICHAEL Timothy why is it why is it you carry that damn thing everywhere?

TIMOTHY I don't know Because .. because it talks to me . like I'm normal Not like I'm no dunce

MICHAEL Do you understand what you're hearing?

TIMOTHY It's news It's . news of things happening here and in Belfast Do . do you understand it, Michael?

MICHAEL No I don't You're no dunce, Timothy You're a fine man

IAN Are you coming, Michael? *(IAN exits)*

TIMOTHY Michael! You're not still angered at me?

MICHAEL. No, Timothy. I'm not angered no more

TIMOTHY. I promise not to go in again

MICHAEL Aye I know you won't *(MICHAEL exits through the UL door TIMOTHY sits and turns on his radio as the lights fade to a blackout)*

As the radio becomes audible, we hear a news report of violence in Ulster (throughout this news report and each news report in this script, the coverage is entirely of violence in Northern Ireland and/or political activities relevant to the situation in Ulster, the specifics of what is being said in the reports are not important to the script, the audience should only be able to notice that violence and political activity is all the news) [See back of script for radio broadcasts]

ACT I

Scene 2

As the lights come up the radio broadcast fades out BRIGITTE
enters through the UL door She takes off her coat, hangs it on
the coat rack and crosses to the desk, downstage left

BRIGITTE. Hello Kate. Kate! Are you there? I'm
home

KATE *(from offstage)* Hello Brigitte. I'm just starting dinner Bring me a whiskey will you? Just a small one

BRIGITTE I'll be there in a minute *(She searches through*
the drawers of the desk for a few moments)

KATE. *(Enters from the kitchen)* I have what it is you're
searching for

BRIGITTE. Then you'll please give it to me.

KATE. That's all your money, Brigitte Don't go and
throw it away

BRIGITTE The money belongs to me. It's not your
approval I'm after

KATE What is it for, Brigitte?

BRIGITTE It's no concern of yours

KATE It's because I love you that I'm concerned. I

knew this was coming again *(She begins to set the dining table She pulls a tablecloth from the breakfront)* He's asked you for money for Keith again. To see your life's savings thrown away on a silly boy the likes of Keith Earl All the money you've been saving for America.

BRIGITTE I want the box, Kate. It's mine. You've no right to have it. Please give it to me. Now, Kate.

KATE I'll not stand by and see a sweet girl lose all she's..

BRIGITTE You'll not try my patience, God have mercy, at this moment. You'll not make me into the devil with curses on you For I haven't the will to control myself. Give me the box

KATE. Brigitte dear, you don't even know if Keith's still alive. There's others have died at Long Kesh..

BRIGITTE. We've had letters, Kate. Michael's heard from him. He says this'd be the final payment. Keith'd get out and then Michael would be willing to leave. This will be the final payment, Kate.

KATE. Aye The final one until next month. Then the price will go up Then there'll be one more thieving dog to pay.

BRIGITTE Then I'll pay that one. And the one after that. Don't you see, Kate? There's no price too high. I have to get away from here before I lose Michael.

KATE. Open your eyes, girl. What is it you're paying for? A man who's in jail where he ought to be. For he did have that nail bomb on him, Brigitte And make no mistake If he comes back to this house he'll keep his nose clean. I won't have my house destroyed again.

BRIGITTE. And you're maybe the most cursed woman

in all the Six Counties You know he's no bomb-thrower
They planted that bomb on him after he was knocked
out.

KATE It was his! And Michael is filling your head with
nonsense I'll not let you throw your money away Forgive
me, child I can't let you have the box

BRIGITTE And you knowing that I want it more than
anything You'll not let me have it?

KATE Because I love you, child You're a better child
than any I've had Someone's got to look after

BRIGITTE For you know it isn't the only money we have
in this world There's more you know There's a great deal
more if we want it And it isn't in my money box

KATE Brigitte   what are you talking about?

BRIGITTE A great deal more And the key to it is
Michael's signature, Kate, and that small piece of paper in
Clancy Trobin's office

KATE Don't be saying such an unkind .

BRIGITTE We'll sell this farm, Kate We'll sell it to get
Keith out of jail and we'll leave for America the next
day

KATE The devil himself

BRIGITTE They'll be here in the week to cart you
away

KATE Stop it, Brigitte

BRIGITTE We'll find you a lovely flat near the roaring
Belfast motorway

KATE Stop this at once I won't listen to

BRIGITTE Of course we won't be able to bury you on
property that isn't ours, but Tom Earl would understand
You'll live out your last days in the bustling city On all the

holidays you can have Ian for a visit and...

KATE. *(She crosses to the breakfront and pulls BRIGITTE's box out from one of the drawers She gives the box to BRIGITTE)* Blessed Jesus, it's the devil himself in my own house The most cruel and evil girl . that any good woman has ever lived with.

BRIGITTE. I'm sorry, Kate, but you're wrong to cross me on this. For you know I've not got my wits about me when it comes to Michael. It's his first wish to have Keith out of jail. He'll never go to America until he's out. I'm sorry, Kate.

KATE. It's only pain and trouble you've had these four years.

BRIGITTE. Oh no, Kate. For I love him so. There's no pain in that.

KATE. I only want you to be happy, Brigitte. It's a poison we're living with. I've lived with it all my life. Sometimes it goes away for awhile but its always returning .. always showing up again It took Tom from me and now it's taking my sons. It's their Dad put them to bed at night with this truth of his And you know how young boys believe every word comes from their Dad. You're descended from the great Hugh O'Neill, the Earl of Tyrone! His truth was maybe a good one, but it's only brought me trouble And you know Brigitte, I was quite a pretty girl. I've told you before, the boys, well, they all were knocking at the door. "You've got it all ahead of you, Kate." my Dad said to me. "A fine life for such a pretty girl." And here I am. With my fine life. Trying to tell you just the opposite Truth for some. Poison for me. It's no fine life you're looking at, Brigitte Not with Tom Earl's truth I feel it here again I wish I could save you from it.

BRIGITTE. We'll be leaving, Kate You'll see Michael says we will I know we will when Keith gets out. I'm thirty years old, Kate. It has to be soon I want to have a child, but not here Not in this country Now Kate . forget your poison! We're celebrating! Claire's coming We'll have a grand time We'll start with a whiskey You'll see There's no poison here at all *(She sees Kate's dress box on the coffee table)* And look at that That's the new dress you told me about

KATE *(She shows it to BRIGITTE)* Aye. Do you like it? Mrs Dougherty says to me "No Christian woman would wear it " The color's not for a widow she says

BRIGITTE And who'd be taking advice from Mrs Dougherty and her the sack of potatoes It's lovely And just your color *(MICHAEL, IAN, and TIMOTHY enter through the UL door)* I was just coming to the garage

KATE Dinner'll be ready as soon as Claire gets here

IAN Don't set for me, Mother I'll be going to Pomeroy Something's come up

KATE "Something's come up!," is it? You're hardly safe in your own home but out in the street they'll take you surely I'll soon have all my boys in the kip It's me and Brigitte will be out to the garage fixing lorries There's a picture Don't go out and ask the British to put you in jail, Ian

IAN I've got to go out, Mother

MICHAEL And Timothy won't be here

KATE Timothy not here? Why not? And his sister coming?

IAN We'll explain later, Mother There's no time now.

KATE. A fine welcome for Claire Half of us not here to see her Don't you be drinking yourself silly with that gang in Pomeroy, Ian Earl And don't any of you have your manners? There's a guest coming tonight. Why don't you do your drinking at home where it's proper?

BRIGITTE. Claire won't mind, Kate. It'll be better anyway We want to make plans for the housing march

KATE. This family used to drink together There's no manners here. Company coming and all the men scattering to the winds. It's the women'll sit and have a pot of tea. That'll be great fun. *(Exits up the stairs)*

BRIGITTE *(Crosses to MICHAEL)* You said £120?

MICHAEL I've got the other eighty

BRIGITTE *(Counts out the money and gives it to MICHAEL)* Thieving dogs I've got it Just barely

MICHAEL Put this in Tim's box, Ian

IAN. It's in the garage. Come on, Tim.

BRIGITTE Timothy, wait. I've got something for you. *(She crosses to her coat on the coatrack and takes a small package from the pocket She crosses to TIMOTHY and gives it to him She sings)*

OH, THE SAILOR WAS A' SINGING
  AS THE LASS LAY IN THE SAND
FOR A GIFT SHE WAS A' BRINGING
  AND SHE PUT IT IN HIS HAND

TIMOTHY A p . pr .. present. For ... for me, is it?

BRIGITTE. Well, open it, Timothy Don't just look at it.

TIMOTHY. A   radio. It's beautiful. I've ... I've got one

already, Brigitte.

BRIGITTE I know you do, for I hear it often enough. This is a special one. Look here... it's got a cord and a plug for your ear so only you can hear it. Now you can listen at night if you want and not have Kate yelling at you from the next room.

TIMOTHY. It's beautiful Thank you.

BRIGITTE. And you can listen on the bus too and not be disturbing no one. Now go on. Do what Michael's told you and be careful The money's for Keith. You'll be careful Maybe we'll have him back soon. You'd like that, wouldn't you?

TIMOTHY I wouldn't. I like the .. b ... bed to myself.

BRIGITTE Aye. Well we'll get you one for your own self, maybe Now, you know what to do?

TIMOTHY. Aye. Michael's told me I'm leaving the money. At ten.

BRIGITTE. Now go. And be careful. *(TIMOTHY and IAN exit through the UL door BRIGITTE crosses to MICHAEL He is sitting on the settee with his feet propped up)* You know what Kate will do with the likes of you if she sees your big feet on her precious table.

MICHAEL. I don't care.

BRIGITTE. Well, and aren't you the cheerful one this evening? Are you tired? You're working too hard.

MICHAEL. I'm not working enough. We've had six lorries the week. It's slow.

BRIGITTE. Well and don't I have some news. Remember I was telling you how last month at the shop Mrs. Bigelow asked for one of us to come to the back and help out in the office. I told her I was good at figures but I was scared to death at what she'd give me And wasn't it easy, Michael! I've been keeping the numbers on all the dresses coming in and going out, and filling out the daily sheets. It's been a few hours each day. So Mrs. Bigelow says to me today, "Brigitte, you're doing a fine job and it's more than I can do. Wouldn't you like to work all the day here?" "I don't know," I said, "For it seems like a lot to do." She knew what I was saying and she says quickly that I'd be making £10 more a week. And you should've seen the girls when I told them! Acting like I was a traitor. Well, and didn't they have a chance? Not a one of 'em came up fast when she mentioned working with figures. £10 more a week, Michael Earl! Just think of that and maybe more later she says!

MICHAEL. And you deserve it, don't you? The prettiest and the smartest. Mrs. Bigelow's no fool. She'll have you opening up the next shop and running it too.

BRIGITTE. I don't know about that but I'm hoping to learn about taking care of all those books And here I am chattering away about the shop and acting like I'm the queen of the May. It's Keith you're worried about, isn't it? I miss him too. I've got no one to tease. There's no one so much fun to tease as Keith.

MICHAEL. It's not just Keith, Brig. It's a dangerous time. You've heard what Mr. Faulkner's doing. Putting men in jail for no reason. They say they're torturing them.

BRIGITTE. How is it a man like that gets to be prime minister? Don't think about it. And don't be worrying.

MICHAEL. They picked up Danny O'Farrell today. Ian's gone to Haverhill Road Station to see him. We don't want

Mother to know You know how she is. It's a bad time, Brig It's not just us I'm worried about. I know you'll hate to hear this, but, I'm thinking they'll not really let Keith out. No matter how much we pay.

BRIGITTE   They have to let him out! The thieving dogs! We've paid nearly £1000! They have to let him out!

MICHAEL   They don't have to do anything and they know it.

BRIGITTE   But there's others got their boys out by paying! Michael, they have to let him!

MICHAEL.   It doesn't matter They'll squeeze until they think they've got all they can get.

BRIGITTE.   Well and they've got it too! They'll have no more from us! *(pause)* Sometimes it seems we won't ever get away from this place

MICHAEL   Just a while longer. We have to be patient. We could have a baby

BRIGITTE   No. No, I'll not have one here It's not right. It's no place for children here. I don't want my child to hate. I'll wait. Or I'll have none

MICHAEL   *(He pulls her onto his lap and holds her)* You'll see how soon it's all over We'll go to America and start a family. You've been so brave these four years. I'm proud of you It's a grand and brave scheme to organize the women.

BRIGITTE   That's Claire's grand and brave scheme I'm just helping I'm just acting like I'm grand and brave Giving myself something to think on Something to do We will go to America, Michael, won't we? Just tell me again that we will

MICHAEL   Aye. We will.

BRIGITTE *(She leans against MICHAEL with her head against his As she sings she takes his hand and runs it along her side)*

OH, THE SAILOR WAS A' SINGING
AS THE LASS LAY IN THE SAND
FOR A GIFT SHE WAS A' BRINGING
(She puts his hand on her breast)
AND SHE PUT IT IN HIS HAND

(She speaks) It's for you I'll be patient, Michael, for I love you more than anything Now I must go and help Kate Call me when Claire gets here. And keep your big feet off Kate's precious table! *(BRIGITTE exits to the kitchen MICHAEL crosses to turn on the radio and then sits in the chair by the fireplace The lights fade to a blackout as the radio broadcast comes up)*

ACT I

Scene 3

*MICHAEL is asleep in his chair The radio broadcast continues
and we hear knocking at the UL door After a moment,
MICHAEL wakes up He looks quickly at his watch, crosses
to turn off the radio and then goes to open the door CLAIRE
enters She carries a handbag and an attaché*

CLAIRE There you are, Michael Earl

MICHAEL. *(He hugs CLAIRE)* Ah, Claire. Good to see
you Good to see you

CLAIRE You've been sleeping you lazy man

MICHAEL I dozed off in my chair Hope you weren't
waiting long Well, and you're looking lovely as always.

CLAIRE *(She removes her coat and hangs it up)* Thank you,
Michael. You're looking fit yourself How've you been?

MICHAEL Fine. Fine Garage is slow, but we're all fine
Yourself? How've you been?

CLAIRE. Very well I keep busy

MICHAEL Aye It's few women could do what you're
doing with the ladies' group

CLAIRE It takes up so much time, Michael. I've been

37

meaning to talk to you about that. I want you to know, and Kate and Ian too, I appreciate your keeping Timothy It's a lot. .

MICHAEL Ah, Claire, you mustn't say that.

CLAIRE Yes, I must. It is a lot to ask of people who aren't his family I'm away from home so much and he'd be all alone It's good for him to be around the men, like you and Ian I know he's better off here

MICHAEL It's nothing Claire Don't give it a thought. Your ladies' group is good for Brigitte too. I'm glad you've got her involved It makes me proud of the both of you Just this evening I was telling her what a brave scheme it is. For there's danger in it. There's Republican women in Andersontown who'd cut your throat.

CLAIRE Aye, I suppose they would I think there's some who want the killing to go on, Michael

MICHAEL. I don't think anybody wants the killing, Claire, just changes Well   ah . . the ladies is in the kitchen *(He starts to exit to the kitchen)* I'll tell them you're..

CLAIRE. Oh ... before you do, Michael. What's the news of Keith?

MICHAEL We had a call just today He might get out soon. Truth to tell we had to send more money. Seems there's more crooked British than honest ones, especially at that prison.

CLAIRE It's costing you a lot, isn't it?

MICHAEL. It is that. Well, let me tell the ladies you're here. *(He yells into the kitchen)* Brigitte! Mother! Claire's here! *(back to CLAIRE)* I'm forgetting my manners. Would you care for a whiskey, Claire?

CLAIRE   That'd be nice

(KATE enters, followed by BRIGITTE KATE is wearing her new
   blue dress They both run to CLAIRE to hug her)

KATE   It's been too long, Claire Strain.
CLAIRE   Kate!
KATE   We thought you'd forgotten us
BRIGITTE   Claire!
CLAIRE.   Brigitte!
BRIGITTE   Don't you look pretty!
KATE.   Isn't she a picture, Brigitte? You've cut your hair!
CLAIRE.   Thank you. I have. You're looking well yourself, Kate
KATE   Oh, the devil! I'm an old woman, Claire Being alive is looking well I've made your favorite tonight.
CLAIRE   Ah! Bless you, Kate. And you the best cook in all the Six.
KATE.   Oh, the devil! Well, maybe it's so Won't you have a whiskey?
CLAIRE   Michael's offered
KATE.   Just a small one for me, Michael You've got to come round more often, Claire. *(She directs them to the settee)* Those speeches on the radio! We're proud of you, young lady.
CLAIRE.   Brigitte's going to help me write some new ones I feel like I'm saying the same old thing and no one listening a'tall.
BRIGITTE.   Me, is it? I won't be much help with public speaking. It's you with the gift of the gab.

CLAIRE   Well I'll be gabbing at Carrickmore on Sunday And several meetings next week in the area. I'll make a pest out of myself coming here for visits

KATE.   You're always welcome in this house. I can't wait to hear all your stories I've got to get back to the cooker Brigitte, you stay and entertain your sister We'll eat soon *(As she is exiting to the kitchen, KATE takes a glass of whiskey from MICHAEL. He pours another one for CLAIRE and takes it to her)*

CLAIRE   And where's my brother Timothy? Not here to greet his next-favorite sister?

MICHAEL   It's Timothy who's gone to take the money for Keith, Claire

BRIGITTE   Oh, Michael's told you about Keith maybe getting out soon! It might be soon, Claire I'm sorry about Timothy not being here You understand We had to send him

CLAIRE   Brigitte, I'm glad I've got you and Michael alone for a moment. Keith's out

MICHAEL   What is it you're saying, Claire? He's at Long Kesh prison

CLAIRE   He's not at Long Kesh

MICHAEL.   He is. Why is it you're saying that?

BRIGITTE.   We've heard from him We just today heard from somebody on the inside. Isn't it so, Michael?

CLAIRE   He's not there I don't know where they've got him, but it's not at Long Kesh

MICHAEL.   What are you saying?

BRIGITTE   Claire. And you the stubborn one. We've had letters from him They've suspended visiting rights but we

MICHAEL   Aye   They haven't let us visit but we've had letters

BRIGITTE   We sent money just today, Claire   One of the guards picks it up from Timothy   The Lacey's had to bribe too   For Pat   They got him out and we're still paying

CLAIRE   There's a clever hoax being played on the both of you   Keith isn't at Long Kesh   He's been gone from there nearly a year

MICHAEL   How do you know that?

CLAIRE   Mary Dunlap told me that she saw him in Monaghan

MICHAEL   She saw him?   Did she speak to him?

CLAIRE   No

MICHAEL   Ah, Claire   She mistook him. She's just seen someone who looks like him   Surely she mis. .

BRIGITTE   Ah! That Mary Dunlap! 'Twas another handsome man caught her eye. And don't I know how she's always looking

CLAIRE   I been asking around, Michael. I'm surprised you haven't checked   Kevin Buchanan just got out of Long Kesh and he says Keith hasn't been there for a good ten months   It's a hoax   They're not allowing visitors because he's not there

BRIGITTE   They told Michael no visitors   I can't believe it   You're sure?

CLAIRE   I'm only sure he's not at Long Kesh.

BRIGITTE   We've spent so much. Nearly £1,000 this year! The thieving dogs! Think of all we've spent, Michael!

MICHAEL   We have   We.. we'll not again. That you can be sure of.

(The telephone rings)

MICHAEL *(Begins to cross to answer phone)* I'll find out where he is. If he's out I'll go to Monaghan myself I'll find out if he's part of this He'll not.

KATE *(Enters from the kitchen and crosses to the phone)* I'll get it.

MICHAEL. If it's Ian I want to speak to him

BRIGITTE He's not I'm sure he's not part of it. He wouldn't do that to us

KATE. *(in the background)* Hello   Aye   He does   Aye Where? I'll tell him

CLAIRE It's probably not Keith taking your money

MICHAEL I'm sure there's some explanation to it, Claire They must've moved him, maybe to one of the bigger prisons. That must be it. They're pretending he's there *(He turns to KATE)* Who was that?

KATE They've arrested Ian

MICHAEL Jesus Christ!

KATE. He's at Haverhill Road Station

MICHAEL Why?! Did they say why?

KATE He was trying to get Danny O'Farrell out of jail The R.U.C. didn't like that.

MICHAEL. Damn! *(He puts on his jacket and starts to leave)*

BRIGITTE Michael, where are you going?

MICHAEL. To get Ian out ... if I can.

BRIGITTE No! Michael, you can't! They'll put you in jail too. They'll keep you too

MICHAEL No, they won't. They'd have come for me if they wanted me It's just up the road They all know me there Don't wait dinner *(He crosses through the UL door)*

BRIGITTE *(Tries to stop him)* I'll come with you

MICHAEL You won't, Brigitte You'll stay here with Claire and Mother And don't worry They won't keep me

BRIGITTE Michael, please don't' Are you so anxious to be in jail too? You're not thinking I'm coming with you

MICHAEL You'll stay quietly and say a prayer for Ian *(He exits)*

BRIGITTE *(She follows him out the door)* Michael' Wait! They'll keep you. Michael, wait! *(She comes back into the room)* They'll keep him I'm afraid they'll.

KATE Brigitte, he's right. They'd have taken him if they wanted him. The R.U C know he's here It's Ian's own fault. Getting involved in something that wasn't his business. Him and that gang in Pomeroy Ian's in it too

BRIGITTE He isn't, Kate!

CLAIRE Brigitte .. could be there's some truth to what Kate's saying

BRIGITTE It's not true' Not a word of it. Michael would never allow it. If Ian's involved you can be sure Michael doesn't know about it.

KATE You're blind, Brigitte You're so much in love with that man

CLAIRE Brigitte. It's possible, you know. I had this feeling that when I was telling Michael about Keith, he knew He knew Keith wasn't at Long Kesh.

BRIGITTE. He couldn't have, Claire. We just sent money He wouldn't He'd not lie to me He's a good man

CLAIRE. Of course he's a good man but there's many

things he .

BRIGITTE He'd never lie to me. You'll both stop this.

KATE Brigitte, listen to your sister Aye, he's got plenty of good in him It's what I've told you about ... their father That poor man passed on his lifetime of lies to his sons Aren't we all clever here? Smiling .. pretending Living day to day, all of us, Brigitte, knowing what not to talk about.

BRIGITTE Kate, I don't want to listen to this.

KATE We none of us want to listen to the truth When we can remember what the truth is. There's a pretty lie we all tell about Tom Earl You've heard it, Brigitte. Shot in the head, trying to get some guns up to the boys in Derry Gave his life for the cause! It was no gunshot killed him. One of his own bombs went off in his face   the fool thing went off in his face! I had to identify the body There wasn't anything left to identify. And now I'm part of the lies too. When Tom died I told them I wouldn't have the IRA in my house. It's banned in this house So it's all done at that pub in Pomeroy. At Danny O'Farrell's. In that garage out there too It's a proper house here. We all pretend Let's stop this lying to ourselves, Brigitte. My Tom didn't talk about it either Not talking is the same as a lie, isn't it? It took Tom from me. And it will take Michael from you. It's still here. You've got to get out. *(pause)* Well, supper's ready and we're none of us in the mood for it. But I'll not be wasting good food. And me the best cook in all the Six Counties! How long is it now, since this family sat at the table together? *(She pours herself a glass of whiskey)* This house was filled with laughter. Would you care for a glass, Claire? Brigitte? There used to be so much laughter

(KATE exits to the kitchen)

CLAIRE Brigitte, I didn't want to hurt you *(She crosses to pick up her attaché case)* We won't discuss this for now We have to make our plans. It's only four weeks now until the march

BRIGITTE What would I do, Claire? What would I do if they put him in jail?

CLAIRE He'll be back.

BRIGITTE. You're both wrong, you know, Claire You'll see When Michael gets home I'll ask him He's not involved. He'd never lie to me

(A scuffing noise is heard outside the UL door)

CLAIRE. Did you hear that? Is someone at the door?
BRIGITTE. Who is it?

(The door bursts open. KEITH enters with his gun drawn He looks around the room)

BRIGITTE Keith!

(The lights go to black immediately)

END OF ACT ONE

ACT II

Scene 1

*As the lights come up we see KEITH, BRIGITTE and CLAIRE
exactly as they were at the end of Act I KEITH puts his hand
to his mouth to indicate that the ladies should be quiet He
puts his gun back into his jacket as he steps back outside the
door to see if he is being followed He comes into the room and
shuts the UL door behind him. He looks from BRIGITTE to
CLAIRE and back to BRIGITTE After a pause, he
speaks*

KEITH. I was hoping there'd be squeals of delight.
(pause) I'd pay dearly for just one squeal. You always loved
a surprise, Brigitte. *(pause)* Didn't you?

BRIGITTE. It's the little boy with the big ears The pride
of the house himself at the door! *(She runs to hug him)*
Keith! Keith! It's a sight I've been waiting for this long
year! Kate! He's here. Your own big ears is here!

KEITH. It's good to see you. And you as mean as the day
you were born! I'll not be listening to names for babies.
I've grown into my ears you know. It's no youngster
standing here.

46

BRIGITTE   Aye An old man I can see. Kate' It's big ears'. He's out!

KEITH   I'd forgotten about the peculiar forms of affection in this house.

BRIGITTE   Keith We're so glad to see you We were beginning to think you'd never get out. We've been so worried And where's your good manners? Claire standing right here and you chatting away like she's your neighbor's goat.

KEITH   Me chatting away is it? I've not had a chance have I? Not with the witch on her broom

BRIGITTE   *(She pushes KEITH over to CLAIRE)* Well take your chance Mr Ears and have a look at the lovely lady. She doesn't squeal mind you But she has a nice smile *(She runs over near the kitchen door)* Kate' Are you coming? There's a surprise'

KEITH   Hello, Claire How are you?

CLAIRE   It's good to see you, Keith

KEITH   You're looking even more lovely than I remembered.

CLAIRE.   There you see, Brig. He's got his manners. He still knows how to flatter the ladies.

BRIGITTE   You're supposed to squeal, Claire. He wants to hear squeals. He said so himself.

(KATE enters from the kitchen)

KEITH.   Hello, Mother

KATE.   I suppose you'll be wanting some supper.

KEITH.   There's a warm greeting. I'd love to have some supper. Don't I get a hug first?

KATE. Supper first A hug later Maybe Take off your coat and hat why don't you? And those muddy boots. You'll be growing potatoes in those filthy things It's a proper house you're in now, little man Do you want to wash up, first? Let me see those dirty hands

KEITH. My hands are clean, Mother

KATE. Brigitte, put a nice whiskey in his hands like it's proper We're glad you're out, Keith I hope you know how to stay out of jail this time And you the lucky one coming here on a night when this lovely lady's here and us not seeing her these long months There's a shortage of men in the house tonight. You'll have three of us to entertain, Mr. Lucky. *(She exits to the kitchen.)*

KEITH. Where's Michael? Was that his lorry I saw racing down the roads not two minutes ago?

BRIGITTE. Aye. It was maybe his He's just after leaving in a big rush.

KEITH. Damn. I knew it was him I would've flagged him but there was other cars on the road.

CLAIRE. The boots, Keith The boots Kate'll make you sorry to be back if you spread any more of that dirt around this house. It looks like you've been in the fields

KEITH. *(He sits to remove his boots)* Well, and I have, haven't I! I've had to walk from Pomeroy and the roads are crawling with British soldiers Right through the muddy fields and me in my best boots! Ruined. Damn! Lifted 'em from a fine shop in Moy too Leather soles. Brigitte, where was Michael off to?

BRIGITTE Pomeroy. He'll be back shortly.

CLAIRE. Is he expecting you, Keith?

KEITH. Hah! Indeed he's not. It's a surprise.

CLAIRE Ah Aye He'll be surprised

KEITH You're sure he'll be back soon? I've got to find him soon He needs to know I'm here

CLAIRE. You're best to wait for him here. You don't want to be seen in Pomeroy do you?

KEITH I don't. And what's all this talk about being out? "Glad you're out."

BRIGITTE Out. Meaning out of prison Out of Long Kesh prison

KEITH Aye I'm out. That's true enough   for I'm right here and glad of it I have to be a mite careful you understand, or I'll be back there. Damn! Crawling through the damn muddy fields And my back half broken from crouching under the seat of a bus We've got a nun, you know She snuck me through all the way Ha ha! She runs guns for us too All through the Six Counties She's got a nice green Volkswagen bus with "St. Patrick's Parish School" written across the side as big as daylight and an unblessed St Christopher magnet medallion stuck like a bull's-eye on the dash She was telling me that monsignor won't bless the medals no more on account of St. Christopher being desainted or made a commoner or a legend or whatever they done to him. But they still have a stock o' these magnet medals in the church stores and they aren't selling. Sister says she carries 'em around and sticks 'em on Unionist cars and army vehicles every chance she gets. Right next to the Ian Paisley stickers Ha ha! A darling old sister. She smiles sweetly at the bloody soldiers and tells 'em how she's praying for peace and all I nearly laughed out loud when I heard her. And me crouched under their very noses. My poor aching back I'll be paying for that ride from Monaghan

CLAIRE It's a tough life, being a terrorist, isn't it, Keith?

KEITH Aye It's tough at times What about another whiskey, Brigitte?

BRIGITTE You've been out? You haven't been at Long Kesh for the past year?

KEITH What are you talking about?

BRIGITTE. When did you get out?

KEITH Out of Long Kesh?

BRIGITTE Aye

KEITH. 'Twas last October I was released I've been in Monaghan since June Was in Dublin before then What's this about getting out?

BRIGITTE. We've just heard from the guard Just today We thought the money was going for you Timothy's taking money Blessed Jesus So much money I don't understand, Keith We got your letter from Long Kesh three weeks ago *(She crosses to the cabinet to get his letter.)*

KEITH What's this about money? Someone is teasing you if you've got a letter from me I've never written to you I might've, but Michael forbade it Right after I got out he sent word that I should stay away from home and shouldn't write a'tall He said it would throw suspicion on him and Ian You're teasing me, Brigitte Is she teasing, Claire?

CLAIRE Show it to him, Brig

BRIGITTE. Michael knows? He knows you've been out?

KEITH. *(He takes the letter from BRIGITTE's hand.)* He does of course. I've had messages from him ... through the boys *(BRIGITTE turns away from KEITH and sits down She stares blankly and only half-listens to CLAIRE and KEITH talking)*

CLAIRE   Released, were you, Keith?

KEITH.   Aye Not before paying a price I had it easy compared to some They only hurt my leg There's some they damaged here. *(He points to his head)* Not me I'm as quick as ever.

CLAIRE   That quick, Keith?

KEITH.   Aye The same as ever *(He reads over the letter)* A hundred pounds! No No, Brigitte That's not mine, I promise you that. Though I'll admit it's a clever likeness. I'd never ask for that kind o' money from my own family, Brigitte. Where would you get it? You've sent the money?

CLAIRE   Nearly £1,000 this last year

KEITH   A thousand! A thousand pounds? I'm sorry . I ... it's . . very clever   . the likeness.

BRIGITTE   Michael knows you've been out?

KEITH.   I think Michael's been trying to protect you, Brigitte. Maybe he's thinking you'd not approve I've heard about your ladies' group Claire and you. I'm not pleased with it, mind you, but it's a good cover for the boys .. I mean .. it's been .. I . . I've heard so much about your ladies' group, Claire You've got a big housing march coming up I read about it. That's fine You're famous

CLAIRE   It's true Surely the most hated woman in all of Northern Ireland.

KEITH.   *(He pours himself another whiskey)* And the most loved if you'd be asking the Unionists. They're probably thinking that the nice Catholic lady from County Tyrone is doing more for them than any guns can do I've heard your speeches on the radio "Ireland! One nation, without bloodshed!" Ha Ha! Good luck with that one! I've even heard it said that you want the ladies to turn over IRA members to the Army. Is that true, Claire?

CLAIRE It's only a rumor It's the Unionists trying to turn everyone against us It's dangerous for you here, isn't it? Especially now Just for being Keith Earl you'd be taken in

KEITH There's plenty o' places to hide Lots of people on our side People who believe in what we're doing

CLAIRE Why is it you're here?

KEITH Plans

CLAIRE. Plans?

KEITH Big plans I don't want to miss They're planning big things

BRIGITTE Who's they? Are you talking about Michael?

KEITH Aye Michael. The whole brigade Only they don't know I'm here to help them. Michael would've said no But I wouldn't have missed it for anything Looks like he'll need me too I've been in Pomeroy. They tell me that Danny O'Farrell was picked up.

CLAIRE Aye Ian too. Just this evening. That's where Michael's gone

KEITH Ian?! Jesus Christ! They took Ian? Christ! Ian Well isn't it nice, now you're telling me? When is it I'd have been made aware of that nice piece of news? The two of you worrying about tricksters from Long Kesh and my own brother in the kip Damn! Michael surely needs me now Faulkner'll be paying for this

CLAIRE   I suppose that's what you're meaning when you say "plans."

KEITH   Faulkner's been on our list for a long time. Since before he was prime minister. We're all living for that. And that's why I'm showing up here this very night. Him and his fine factory in Cookstown will be making some nice smoke and him fueling the flames if our luck is with us.

CLAIRE   When are these plans going to happen?

KEITH   Tomorrow. First thing in the morning. He's going to be at that shirt factory. Danny's got it wired. It's all set. Except for Danny *(He toasts CLAIRE)* Here's to you, Claire Strain. I've missed you. A famous lady now. Not had much time to be thinking about me, have you?

BRIGITTE. *(to herself)* A thousand pounds. He's been lying to me *(She begins to softly sing as she stands and crosses the room)*

FOR A GIFT SHE WAS A' BRINGING
AND SHE PUT IT IN HIS HAND
(She speaks) I've been paying for the IRA, Claire *(She turns to KEITH and bangs her fists on his chest. He grabs her hands to protect himself)* Damn! All that money for you and the boys, Keith. How does that make you feel? Are you proud? Did I pay for the gun you're carrying? It's a clever thing isn't it? Fooling a hardworking shopgirl by making promises about leaving this place. Him the lying fool. Taking my money. He'd never go to America.

KEITH   I thought you knew, Brigitte. I thought Michael had told you as soon as you were married. He said he was going to. He's been trying to protect you, Brigitte.

BRIGITTE   Protecting me? Protecting me, is it? He's

been using me And laughing at me Kate was right about this place There's no escaping it   if you stay here So, I'll not be staying I won't stay here and be a cover I'll start planning my own move to America. I'll stay with you, Claire? For now? And Timothy?

CLAIRE. Of course

BRIGITTE You'll have to help me I'm not so strong, you know It'd be hard to be away from him Will you help me pack some things for Timothy?

CLAIRE Aye

BRIGITTE I've been paying money for you, Keith To help get you free Maybe to have them treat you a little better You weren't even there Now I see why it is Michael kept us from trying to visit you or write to you Clever man He had an answer for everything. A lie for everything. What is it I've been paying for, Keith? Does it make you proud?

KEITH I'm sorry, Brigitte.

BRIGITTE. Are you? I wonder if Michael'll be sorry when I leave. There's the question. *(She exits up the stairs.)*

KEITH You haven't answered me, Claire Have you been thinking about me? Have you missed me?

CLAIRE. No. I haven't missed you. I've only thought of you these last few moments coming through that door and bringing in all the bad news. And in the same breath bragging how you're here to murder someone You're a fine man to look at, Keith And to touch. Any woman would miss that in a man. But out of the bed you're a boy. A boy playing guns and war Somehow, in your brothers it's more .. believable

(KATE enters from the kitchen.)

CLAIRE   Kate I'm sorry All your hard work and none of us in the mood for food this night

KATE   Don't you worry about it

CLAIRE   You haven't really talked to your mother yet, Keith Ask her if she's missed you I've heard it's required for mothers *(She exits up the stairs)*

KEITH   It's not the homecoming I'd expected Do I get that hug now?

KATE   Stay there I don't want to be hugging a man whose only come home so he can be in on a murder plot. Voices carry in this old house and it's no surprises I've heard I prayed you wouldn't get involved. In the old days when I used to pray You look fine, Keith At least you're a handsome murderer

KEITH   You're laughing at me, Mother

KATE.   I am. And at all of us I've just made a fine meal and no one's noticed No use setting a grand table for the two of us I'll make us both a plate and we'll sit in the kitchen like we always did

KEITH   That'd be fine I'm starved is what I am

KATE   Do you remember? How it was always me and you in the kitchen After everybody else was up and gone You and me sitting there eating still And talking The rest of 'em gulping down their food and then   gone

KEITH   Aye.

KATE   You'll tell me all about Dublin *(She crosses to the cabinet to pour a glass of whiskey)* First we'll have just a sip to toast your coming home I used to visit there as a girl, you know Every summer my mother and I

(MICHAEL runs in through the UL door)

KATE   Oh, Michael You'll join us won't you, for a toast to Keith's return?

MICHAEL   (*He sees KEITH*) Jesus Christ! Keith!

KEITH   (*He crosses to MICHAEL. They hug*) Michael It's good to see you I've missed you, brother

MICHAEL   Keith   you   how is it you're here   what are you doing here   we only just heard from   the guard today

KATE   You needn't pretend, Michael We all know what's happening It's more of a mess than any of us is prepared for (*She crosses to MICHAEL and hands him a whiskey*) This will help Here's to Keith A boy who's a waste, but at least he's home Now Are you hungry, Michael? Keith and I are going to have a nice plate

MICHAEL   No, mother

KATE   Keith, talk to your brother I'm sure he'll have a load of questions for the likes o' you I'm going to eat If anyone cares to join me you'll bring yourself into the kitchen (*She exits to the kitchen.*)

MICHAEL   I told you not to come here Dammit, Keith! Brigitte   where's Brigitte   and Claire? Have they seen you? They're here?

KEITH   It's not my fault, Michael I didn't know You should've told me what you were doing. I could've pretended the money helped to get me out. I didn't know

MICHAEL   Damn Now they know, don't they? They know you've been out? You told them?

KEITH   I didn't know! You should've told me

MICHAEL   Damn! I didn't know I was doing it. It just happened that's all And it worked so we kept doing it We needed the money Brig had it all saved up Why is it you don't listen, Keith? I told you not to come here It's good to see you, brother, but why is it you're always leading the way for disaster?

KEITH I didn't know Why didn't you tell me?

MICHAEL I haven't got time to talk. *(Removes his outer shirt and crosses to the coat rack upstage He takes a black sweater from the rack and puts it on)* There's things to be done right away And here you are bringing in more trouble

KEITH You'll need my help now With Danny in jail And Ian? What's happened with Ian? I'm here to help you I've missed being here I want to help

MICHAEL Well, you've made a bad start. You don't belong in any brigade You've shown you don't know how to follow orders You talk too much You don't know when to shut up It's no kid game, you know You just don't know how it's done

KEITH I've learned, Michael I don't talk no more

MICHAEL You're here, aren't you? Brigitte knows what we've been doing? It shows you don't know how to follow orders

KEITH Maybe it's the orders I'm getting Michael. "Stay away " "Keep out of sight." "Keep a lookout." Little brother orders Is it all I'm ever going to be in this family?

MICHAEL It's maybe because I don't want you getting killed Did you ever think of that? I promised Dad I'd look after you

KEITH I was a boy then I'm not a boy no more and you're not my dad. No one's asking you to be my dad. I only want to be your brother I don't want protecting.

MICHAEL All right, little brother All right, Keith
Now's maybe the time You could save me some time in
Cookstown tonight Without Danny and without Ian I'll
need some help

KEITH Ian! What do you mean, without Ian?

MICHAEL The R U.C's holding him I couldn't get
him out. You'll be taking a chance If you're seen they'll
arrest you That's for sure

KEITH Do you want to try without them? Can we still
do it without them?

MICHAEL Aye We can do it.

KEITH You don't sound sure

MICHAEL. Nothing's for sure, is it? I don't know nothing anymore I don't know if the voice I hear talking is
my own or Dad's or Ian's maybe Get your coat Are you
going in your stocking feet?

KEITH *(He crosses to sit and put on his boots)* My boots are
ruined. Covered with mud My best boots Leather soles
I lifted 'em from a shop in Moy

MICHAEL You did what? Lifted 'em?

KEITH When I passed through Moy

MICHAEL You say it like you're proud of it, Keith Earl.
Since when is it anyone in this family stole things? You
should be ashamed of it, not bragging about it

(BRIGITTE enters from the stairs)

BRIGITTE Proud of me, is it, Michael?
MICHAEL Brigitte . . I . I'll explain...

(CLAIRE enters from behind BRIGITTE)

CLAIRE Michael You'd better cancel those plans you have in Cookstown for the morning It's only fair that I warn you

MICHAEL Jesus Christ, Keith! Why is it I should cancel my plans, Claire?

CLAIRE I've got no liking for Brian Faulkner, but I'll not have his blood on my hands I'll be calling the R.U C to go to that factory

MICHAEL Ah It's your true self I'm seeing now, Claire I heard that you wanted the ladies to turn the men in It's the Orangemen setting you up, is it? Well, I hope it's a lot of Protestant money they're passing on to you It's not this phone you'll be using *(He pulls the phone cord out of the wall)*

CLAIRE Michael, I'd never turn you in, but I will go and warn them

MICHAEL You'll be staying right here, Claire Neither of you will be leaving this room 'til I get back. Your guard is standing right here *(He turns to KEITH)* You said you wanted to help You've caused this problem Now you'll solve it. See if you can do this right. You'll see he's bigger than the both of you   and I'm certain   that. *(He searches KEITH and pulls a gun from KEITH's jacket)*   yes   yes   he's armed Of course he'd never shoot to kill you, but he knows how to stop someone from running to the authorities, don't you, Keith? He knows surely that they'd kill Michael Earl if they caught him trying to blow up the prime minister, and he knows he'd be next. He knows he and his brothers have been waiting for this for years and that his ol' Dad will be crying in his grave if his boys fail at this For, you see ladies, the death of Brian Faulkner is more important than the lives of us in this room And I'll do it alone if I have to

CLAIRE It's an evil thing, Michael You've lost your mind

MICHAEL Evil? Aye Keith can tell you about evil, Claire Tell the ladies how they clubbed Frank O'Kane to death at Long Kesh, Keith Tell them where they put the electric wires before they clubbed him Tell them what a man screaming out in pain sounds like   if it's evil they want to hear

CLAIRE You haven't convinced me, Michael I don't believe you've convinced yourself either

BRIGITTE It's Claire and me you're so proud of, is it? Using us, that's what you've been doing And taking all of my money All that money for our move to America And you never meaning to go a'tall Lying to me *(She slaps him)*

MICHAEL I'm sorry, Brigitte I had to lie for you'd not have allowed it You're against us in this You've made that clear You're only thinking of yourself Will you have your own house with nice lace curtains? And won't it be perfect with a girl and a boy? The Earl family'll be so nice and lovely Me Us Is that where your vision stops, Brigitte? And there's a whole country here being screwed by the British Empire And them being gone someday, we've got the filthy Protestants laughing at us when we try for the good jobs There's none for us here' You'd best remember you're a lowly Catholic woman You're second class in Ulster and this old farmhouse is as good as we'll ever get.

BRIGITTE And that'd be fine too, with a family and

MICHAEL   Ah But you've got the solution, don't you?
It's so easy We'll just leave County Tyrone We'll go to
America We can stay with your cousin in . . what's it
called   the Bronx is it? That'll be lovely You'll be a clerk
in some store and I'll be a mechanic We'll become Americans So what if this family's been here in County Tyrone
these last thousand years So what if this farm belonged to
my Dad and his Dad before him back to the Earl of
Tyrone That's no reason to fight for anything is it? It's
easy We'll go to America There's a grand thing to do!
There's a life for an Irishman! There's standing a silly-
headed woman We've got work we have to do *(MICH-
AEL exits through the UL door KEITH stands near the UL door
with the gun in his hand There is a pause before CLAIRE
speaks)*

CLAIRE   The nail bomb was yours, wasn't it, Keith?

KEITH   It was I had a good use for it, but I was knocked
out It was meant for a bunch of murdering British
soldiers

CLAIRE   You've changed, Keith

KEITH. It's you who's changed, Claire Thinking you
can solve all this country's problems with your pretty
words.

CLAIRE   And you're going to solve the problems by killing the prime minister? And then there'll be more killing
And the whole thing starts over bigger next time When
does it end, Keith?

KEITH   When the Six is part of Ireland And when the
British get out

BRIGITTE   And just look at what this cause has done to
this family I'm wondering who's getting hurt more The

Orangemen? Or us? Did you ever think you'd be standing there pointing a gun at Claire and me, Keith?

KEITH. You know I'd not shoot you But you'll be staying here I'll not let Michael be caught

CLAIRE You've changed so much, Keith.

BRIGITTE No He's not changed. It's in all of them. I've been fooling myself I've been telling myself Michael maybe had a few friends in the IRA That maybe he knew some of the men who was active in it I've been closing my eyes to what I didn't want to see. And him the Provisional itself

(KATE enters from the kitchen. When KEITH sees her he quickly puts his gun back into his jacket)

KATE. I've put away the supper It's a grand party we're having isn't it?

CLAIRE Keith's not here to come home, Kate. Not here to see the likes of us He's here for some big Provisional plans. He's been out of jail these last.

KATE I've heard all of this, Claire. Seems I've heard it all before, anyway. Claire. Get your coat. You'll have to drive to a telephone in Pomeroy.

KEITH. There'll be no going anywhere, Mother.

KATE Don't you dare to call me "Mother." I've changed my mind. I don't care to be your mother. I always go soft for my boys but I'm not feeling so soft these days. It's no son o' mine would plant a nail bomb to hurt innocent people. Get your coat, Claire

KEITH. Just stay there, Claire.

KATE. Hurry now, Claire. There's not much time. *(She*

pulls out a gun and points it at KEITH)

CLAIRE Kate!

KEITH. Guns, is it, Mother? Guns!? You're not fooling me

KATE Claire, get your coat!

KEITH You're teasing me You'd not shoot me,
Mother

KATE Who was it just now standing here pointing a
gun at us? Your father was right about me needing protecting. But until this day I never knew I'd have to protect
myself from my own sons

KEITH I'd not shoot.

KATE. I will, Keith Earl! Claire!

KEITH. *(He begins to cross toward KATE)* Give me that
gun, Mother

*(The gun fires KEITH screams out and falls to the floor His gun
falls from his jacket onto the floor next to him CLAIRE and
BRIGITTE rush to KEITH KATE puts down her gun She
crosses to help CLAIRE and BRIGITTE with KEITH and
she kicks his gun out of the way, across the floor next to the
radio KEITH continues to cry out in pain throughout the
scene The women yell at each other to be heard)*

CLAIRE Brigitte, help   to the chair Keith, put your
arms... Kate, get some towels and some cold water
(CLAIRE and BRIGITTE move KEITH to the chair)

KATE Use my apron One of you get to a phone.

CLAIRE. Brigitte, you go Take my car. The keys are in
my bag. Just make the call quick and don't identify
yourself.

KATE Brigitte, go!

KEITH No! Claire Brig! Michael   you   can't

CLAIRE Yes, Keith, we can

KATE Sit still and stop moaning

BRIGITTE Claire   it's Michael

KEITH Think of Michael

CLAIRE Aye Think of Michael like he thinks of you Do you want me to go? I'll go Kate, keep pressure

BRIGITTE No I'll. I'll go *(BRIGITTE runs out the UL door)*

KEITH Somebody's got to warn Michael!

(The lights fade immediately to a blackout as a news report fades in)

ACT II

Scene 2

It is very early morning CLAIRE is asleep on the sofa As the news report fades, BRIGITTE enters through the UL door and crosses to hang up her coat CLAIRE wakes up when BRIGITTE accidently drops her keys

CLAIRE Brigitte Where were you? Did you get to a phone?

BRIGITTE I did. I . . I .. wasn't... I wasn't able, Claire. I tried... I couldn't.

CLAIRE. You didn't . . You didn't call?

BRIGITTE. I'm sorry, Claire, I couldn't. I tried.

CLAIRE. I asked you. I asked you if you wanted me to go Do you realize what it is you've done, Brigitte? If that man is killed, we're responsible

BRIGITTE I'm sorry..

CLAIRE You're sorry and maybe the Prime Minister dead. I could've gone. I would've called.

BRIGITTE Well and you should have. It's more to do than you're thinking it is

CLAIRE. They have got to be stopped, Brigitte. We can't

65

be letting them use a gun each time it suits 'em If that man is killed .

BRIGITTE   Will you stop it, Claire Listen to yourself It's no different than Michael standing there talking about the cause and what has to be done

CLAIRE   It's not the same

BRIGITTE   It's the same coming from the other side It's only when I was on my way I started thinking what it was I was being sent to do Tell the R U C. what's happening so maybe they can go there and get my husband for a slow death in Long Kesh prison And that for Brian Faulkner? I'll tell the truth, Claire Strain I'd not shed a tear for that man. I love Michael, Claire He's been good to me

CLAIRE   Aye He's good to you when he's not stealing your money or lying to you Is it "good" he is in the privacy of your bed at night?

BRIGITTE. And that maybe not such a bad kind of goodness You'd not be interested in that, I know We're so different, you and me, Claire. I like looking after the men. I'm not meant to be part of the ladies' group.

CLAIRE   You should've told me to go

BRIGITTE. I didn't know I couldn't I was angry at being lied to. I wanted to get back.   I'm not strong, Claire..

CLAIRE. It's too late now, isn't it? I ... I should have gone myself.

BRIGITTE. I'm not strong, Claire.

CLAIRE. Never mind I'm sorry for asking you to go (pause) Where've you been?

BRIGITTE   Driving. I've been to St. Joseph's church in Donaghmore I just drove and ended up there. We were married there.

CLAIRE Aye. I know.

BRIGITTE. I. . I sat there asking Him questions, Claire. One question after another And I waited quietly for an answer. He used to answer me so quickly. I'd ask. . and then a moment later I'd hear His answer. I was sitting there in the dark and I knew it'd shortly be getting light. I knew I could just ask Him all my questions and the answers would fall right down on me just as soon as the sun hit those colored-glass windows So I just sat and waited, Claire. And then .. then the sun came and in came streaming all those shafts of blue and red .. and .. gold .. and I looked for my answers .. in those shafts of light falling on the floor I looked for my answers. But .. there wasn't any I saw just shafts of colored light .. and no answers there a'tall. So I asked again .. and listened. It's the first time, Claire. He didn't answer me. Maybe the questions is harder this time.

CLAIRE You're going to have to make some decisions. On your own. What will you do . if .

BRIGITTE. If he isn't in jail by now? If he isn't dead. I'll stay. And try to get him to leave this place. I can't leave him even though I hate his being . in the Provisional. I love him too much. There's worse things to live with. He's just a man believing too much in something. He believes in his cause, Claire. I wonder if that's not something good. Maybe it's us is wrong *(pause)* How's Keith? Where is he?

CLAIRE He'll be all right. We've loaded him up with whiskey and put him to bed. It's only a bad surface wound

BRIGITTE. Were you glad to see him, Claire?

CLAIRE Aye I didn't want to be glad. And I didn't know I'd be glad until he walked through that door tonight. I was a lot younger two years ago. I don't know if I loved him He was there when I needed someone. We had ... a nice time together. Then his damned nail bomb made me realize

BRIGITTE. Did you talk about . the two of you?

CLAIRE. A bit. He's such a boy, Brig. I don't think he'd ever give up his IRA And I'd never marry into it. So, there's not much to talk about

BRIGITTE. You've got courage, Claire.

CLAIRE That's just what I don't have. It's fear I've got. A monstrous great fear of losing a man. A fear of even loving a man It's you with the courage. Staying on with Michael Knowing that . that you might be seeing him only on visiting days if he lands in the kip like so many do.

BRIGITTE. I'm thinking that I might have a child now Maybe then he'll see we should leave I'll be damned sure that child doesn't hear stories about the "cause"

CLAIRE You've wanted a child for so long Maybe that would help

(KATE enters from the stairs)

KATE Brigitte, where've you been?

CLAIRE. *(Gestures for KATE not to ask BRIGITTE any questions She changes the subject)* How's Keith?

KATE Gone to sleep, finally Moaning the whole time of it. He's a great baby when it comes to pain It's a fine mother I am, isn't it? Shooting her own boy *(She starts to exit to the kitchen)* Well, I'll be making some tea. Are you.

(TIMOTHY runs in through the UL door)

KATE   Timothy! *(TIMOTHY stands just inside the door He is very dishevelled and there is some dried blood visible on his sweater After a pause, CLAIRE and BRIGITTE rush to him.)*

BRIGITTE   Timothy' What . are you all right? You're bleeding Claire he's bleeding' Kate,   call the doctor

TIMOTHY   No . no doctor

CLAIRE   Timothy, what's happened to you?

BRIGITTE   He's hurt, Claire. Kate,   . the doctor .

KATE   You're forgetting the phone's out, Brigitte

TIMOTHY   I'm not . not hurt, Claire. I'm not   not. . *(He crosses into the room and sits The women all follow him)*

BRIGITTE.   Timothy, where've you been? You went to Stephen's?

TIMOTHY   I   been . I been to Antrim Road .. I been to . wait .. for the ... bus

BRIGITTE.   Aye, Timothy That I know. You took the money for Keith, on the way to Stephen's You can tell me . what happened?

TIMOTHY   I   was   waiting 'til . t . . ten

BRIGITTE.   You were waiting for the bus, Timothy . with the money

TIMOTHY   They . they   tried to kill me, Brigitte

CLAIRE   Who? Who tried to kill you, Timothy?

TIMOTHY   'Twas Ian . and   and Michael They tried to kill me It wasn't no bribe money I was waiting 'til ten, but I couldn't wait no more I had to go to the W.C I had

to go and I couldn't wait no more I left the box so   so the
man could take it if he was there 'Twas no bribe money
'Twas no . never any before   either I   been   murdering people I been killing I think   I knew it .
before

CLAIRE No Timothy It wasn't your money box
that.

BRIGITTE What are you saying, Timothy? How did
this happen?

TIMOTHY. I was in the   W C   and I heard a great
explosion . and people was screaming   and I knew I
done it And I came out and started to run away Then
then   there was a man called   out   for help A great
large man I went to help.. and.. and when I bent down
to him . the man ... was still . . alive . though his chest
was blown a-wide open. He   he was holding . a baby
a boy   and he . the man   says to me   "take him. . sir"
he says So I   I   took him   I took him 'cause I knew
... I knew you'd . care .. for him, Brigitte But   but I left
him   then I left him 'cause . . 'cause I seen   he was
dead. I've lost   my radio, Brigitte. my new radio They
tried   to kill me.

CLAIRE You mustn't say that, Timothy!

TIMOTHY They wanted to kill me because I.. I . know
about . their room   their secret room.

KATE What room is that, Timothy?

TIMOTHY Their room . their secret room

BRIGITTE. What is it you're saying, Timothy? Where is
that room?

TIMOTHY Under. the g   g   the garage At the back
under the g .. garage.

BRIGITTE   How is it you know that? Who told you such a thing?

TIMOTHY.   I was there   Ian found me there   He and Michael was angered at me. They tr .. tried to kill me.

BRIGITTE   He's answered me now, Claire   No shafts of colored light. Just clear answers   Timothy, Kate's just starting tea and I know she'll make you some breakfast. You must be hungry   And look at you   You're a mess   Are you all right? Are you sure you're all right? This room's under the garage? At the back?

TIMOTHY   It's hid   It's under the floor   You   have .. have to move the bench   and   and there's a latch

KATE   Come on, Timothy   We'll have a nice breakfast and get you cleaned up   *(KATE takes TIMOTHY and they exit to the kitchen)*

BRIGITTE   *(as she crosses to put on her coat)*   Claire, listen and see if there's any news about Faulkner   Or about the bomb in Antrim Road

CLAIRE   Where are you off to?

BRIGITTE   I'll be out to the garage for a few minutes . to have a look at this .. "secret room"   *(BRIGITTE exits through the UL door   CLAIRE crosses to turn on the radio)*

(A radio broadcast fades in as the lights fade to a blackout)

ACT II

Scene 3

KEITH is sitting in the chair, stage left The radio broadcast continues CLAIRE is inspecting KEITH's leg which is propped up on a footstool KATE enters

KATE. Will you have some breakfast, Claire? *(She turns off the radio)* We've heard enough of that, haven't we?

CLAIRE Is it hurting, Keith? I'll send Timothy for the doctor

KATE There's no need of that, Claire He's a great baby *(She inspects KEITH's leg He moans)* Oh, shut up! It's only the surface He'll be fine inside two days It's not for nothing your father taught me to shoot, Keith It's a good thing I'd not been drinking

KEITH Your own son...

KATE Not my own! I've told you, I don't care to be related to you I've disowned you until it suits me to take you back It's no son of mine that comes home for a murder plot

(BRIGITTE enters through the UL door She crosses to the desk,

downstage left, and locks up the book she is carrying.)

KATE Ah, Brigitte, won't you have some breakfast?

BRIGITTE No, thank you, Kate. Maybe some tea?

KATE. *(She crosses toward the kitchen.)* I'll get it. Claire?
(CLAIRE shakes her head.)

KEITH I'll have a cup, mother

KATE And a biscuit?

KEITH Aye *(KATE exits to the kitchen.)* Shooting her own
son! And me the only one who'd ever listen to her old
Dublin stories.

BRIGITTE. How's your leg, Keith? *(She inspects KEITH's
leg.)*

CLAIRE Kate says he's fine. It's only the surface.

KEITH. Only the surface! You're the brave one with a
hole in my leg

BRIGITTE. Aye. Now it's stopped bleeding it's not so
bad. It's only scraped you, Keith. And you acting like it's
your death throes

KEITH And how would you like it? Hand me my
gun, Claire

BRIGITTE Oh! Claire . the radio

CLAIRE Faulkner cancelled his Cookstown appearance No explanation.

KEITH And I'll probably be thrown out of this house
and the lads'll have nothing to do with me

CLAIRE Is that so terrible, Keith?

BRIGITTE Any news on Antrim Road? The bomb?

CLAIRE. It's ugly news.

*(TIMOTHY enters. He is drying a dish which he puts into the
breakfront.)*

BRIGITTE *(She changes the subject so that TIMOTHY won't hear)* Oh, Claire Didn't you want some tea? Timothy, will you go tell Kate that Claire would like some tea, too?

TIMOTHY You don't want me to hear I know what you're talking about I heard you I know I killed those people Did you hear what I done Keith?

BRIGITTE *(She tries to put her arm around TIMOTHY)* Timothy, it wasn't you Don't be saying that

TIMOTHY *(He pulls away from BRIGITTE)* It was me carried the box I done . . that before Did you know that, Keith?

KEITH No, Timothy Never before And it wasn't you responsible for last night

TIMOTHY I know It was Ian and Michael And now I'm not supposed to hear no one . talking about it. But I heard *(He pulls out his old radio)* I've got my old radio *(He holds up the radio proudly)* There's ways to hear everything, Brigitte. *(He crosses to KEITH)* My bike's blown up, Keith I can't fix it, like you showed me

KEITH We'll get you a new one then.

TIMOTHY In Moy?

KEITH Aye I've got connections there

TIMOTHY *(He crosses on his way to the kitchen)* Still want that tea, Claire? *(He exits to the kitchen)*

CLAIRE There's sixteen badly hurt and four dead

BRIGITTE God forgive us

(MICHAEL runs in quickly through the UL door)

MICHAEL. *(He removes his jacket and hurls it at the coat rack)*

All our plans wasted! He cancelled Cookstown   Cancelled! Jesus Christ! More wasted plans *(He crosses to KEITH)* Looks like he had a warning

(KATE enters from the kitchen)

MICHAEL   Is it two women proved too much for the likes o' you? What do you think Dad would think of his boys today, Keith?

KATE   It was three women against Keith, Michael Earl And the third one had a gun And she put a nice hole there in his leg just to stop his foolishness Would you care for some breakfast?

(TIMOTHY enters from the kitchen   He crosses to MICHAEL)

MICHAEL   Timothy .   you.

BRIGITTE   It's all so ugly, Michael. You haven't killed Brian Faulkner, but your bomb in Antrim Road has killed four so far   There's sixteen badly hurt

MICHAEL   Brigitte .

BRIGITTE.   And probably not one of 'em British or in the R.U C   And you haven't killed Timothy like you and Ian wanted   He left your "money" box to go to the W C   and when he came out there was dying people all around   It's all so ugly, Michael

MICHAEL   Brigitte, will you please

BRIGITTE.   Now it's all of us know about your little room under the garage. It's a nice hoax you've played on me

MICHAEL   I've wanted to tell you, Brigitte   You just won't listen   I know I've done things wrong. Brigitte,

you'd never understand that there's things need chang-
ing. Things that won't change without violence.

BRIGITTE Violence, is it? Violence, I don't understand? And what it can do? As if I haven't seen enough of
it. As if we all haven't You're the one who doesn't understand, Michael We all know a lot about violence. We can
tell anyone about bombs and flying glass and guns and
screaming children and how much blood pours out of a
man with a bullet hole in his head Timothy can tell us
about a man's chest blown open Kate can tell us what it
was like to try to identify the man they said was your dad
The violence is easy We're the world's living, breathing
experts on violence It's in charge here Not Brian Faulkner Not the British Army It's violence runs this country
And the thing we all know best about it is that it helps
nothing and that it's not going away And I know that. I
can't win against it So it's me who's leaving.

MICHAEL Why is it you can't understand? It's different
for a man He's got things he has to do with his life Don't
you remember my Dad

BRIGITTE Did you think I didn't know? Did you think a
woman could live with a man she loves and not see the
hate all over him? It's true enough I didn't see the
guns

MICHAEL Brigitte, will you please shut up about
those guns

BRIGITTE And what a great hoard o' guns it is in your
hidden room Keith, you'd be proud It's a stack as high as
a man's head All kinds o' guns, and explosives, and
and something like a rocket gun o' some kind they're putting together and I don't know what all. This old farm's an

arsenal, Kate. This old farm is it, Kate! Right here in Tom
Earl's garage is the place where everything comes in for all
the Provisional in Northern Ireland We are it! And I've
found a book that shows how it gets here Wait 'til you see
what the boys've been up to in their secret room You'll be
so proud. Aye, Michael I knew about your Dad. And I
maybe knew you'd be a part of it too But I didn't know
where and what you were doing I didn't want to know
But I knew if I could get you away from here some of the
hate in those great blue eyes of yours would fade away
(pause) I want it back. You'll give it all back to me, Michael
Now I know where all my money's gone and I want it
back. £1,000 And quickly I'll be needing that money to
go to America. With Timothy

    MICHAEL   You'll not be going to America.
    BRIGITTE   I will And you'll be helping me
    MICHAEL   You're staying here

*(IAN enters through the UL door He stands just inside the door as
    he takes a look around the room)*

    IAN   Here's quite a gathering *(He turns to MICHAEL)* I
heard he cancelled Cookstown
    MICHAEL.   How'd you get out? They wouldn't even let
me know where you were
    IAN   They let me go after questioning *(He looks at TIM-
OTHY as he crosses to KEITH)* And look who's here I'm
glad you could make it little brother Ah You've had
some trouble I see
    KEITH   Mother's my trouble
    BRIGITTE   It's good you're here, Ian Both of you will

have to help It's your whole brigade will have to help.
You'll need £1,000, and quickly

MICHAEL   Brigitte, you'll stop this now. I'll not allow
this

BRIGITTE   Ian, you'll be glad to know, I've just spent an
interesting hour in that new underground room of yours.
Stacks o' guns and there's a book filled with details on
purchases, and contacts, and there's names and places all
through it. It's no wonder you know so much about the
Bronx, Michael Seems you get a lot of help from certain Americans

IAN   Michael .. what's happening here? She's got
our book.

MICHAEL   Brigitte, it's me who's the head of this house.
You'll have to listen to me .

BRIGITTE   That's just what I won't be doing, Michael.
It'd not be wise would it? A man who'd lie and take all my
money. A man who'd kill my own brother

IAN.   Michael, she's got our ledger

BRIGITTE.   Aye. And you haven't got much time if you
want it back.

IAN.   Michael, it's your wife's got our ledger book. Ask
your wife to give it to you

MICHAEL   Brigitte you'll be giving us that. .

KATE.   You both heard her You'll repay Brigitte her
money and then you'll have your book.

MICHAEL.   Brigitte . . we'll get you the money It'll take
some time, but we'll get it ..

IAN.   Michael, it's your wife .

MICHAEL.   Brigitte   just give us the book.

BRIGITTE   Get out. Both of you. And come back with
my...

IAN Give me the book, Brigitte.

BRIGITTE Get out

IAN Who is it telling me to get out of my own house?
Not the wife of my brother, is it? Well, I'm laughing at
that And it's me telling her to get out. You're not thinking, Brigitte You're not realizing that the Earl family has
certain beliefs they're entitled to It's you who came into
this house long after the men here belonged to the IRA
And I'm sorry that you don't like that. I'm even sorrier
that Michael didn't tell you about it before he married
you He thought it'd be best to protect you It's not going
to change here, Brigitte It's you should be leaving

BRIGITTE You're right, Ian It's no place for me in this
house It's no place for my brother We're worth nothing
to your cause You have to be willing to die to be in this
family I believe in your cause But not enough to die
for it.

IAN You don't even know what a cause is. You and
Claire have got it figured out, don't you? You've got it
solved You'll plan a housing march. Maybe a boycott of
some Protty's food market. And when things take an ugly
turn at the Divis Flats you'll get really serious and get up a
protest petition

BRIGITTE Get out, Ian

IAN That'll show 'em In no time a'tall   a hundred
two hundred years we'll have results *(pause)* Don't tell me
you believe in my cause, Brigitte. You don't even know
what it is.

KATE Get out of this house, Ian We've had enough of
your cause here

IAN Won't be our house for long, Mother. This farm's

almost gone Everything's been sold just to keep food on
that table An old garage A half acre where Dad's buried.
And this old house. That's all that's left. Fixing lorries
doesn't pay, Mother. And even if it did, it's Michael does
most of that. He's going to America. What'll we do to keep
this house? Had enough of *my* cause, Mother? *(He turns to
BRIGITTE)* It's our Dad died for Ireland and we just
might have to do that too. In the meantime, there's things
to be done and I'll need that book. *(He looks around at each
person in the room)* It looks like I'll have to get it myself. Is it
in your desk? *(He pushes BRIGITTE out of the way and starts
pulling on the desk drawers)*

BRIGITTE *(She crosses upstage and quickly grabs KEITH's
gun from the floor next to the radio and points it at IAN)* Get away
from there, Ian

KEITH. Leave it, Ian. She's got my gun!

CLAIRE Brigitte No! Not a gun

MICHAEL Brigitte .

BRIGITTE Get out, the both of you

MICHAEL Brigitte, you're not thinking clearly You're
not. .

BRIGITTE Aye Maybe I'm not thinking as clearly as I
should. But for once I'm thinking on my own. I'm not
waiting for somebody else to do it for me like I've done my
whole life. And it's sure not going to be the men in this
family does my thinking for me.

MICHAEL Ian. let's go. We'll get the book later. We'll all
talk later when we've calmed down .

KEITH. Ian leave it!

BRIGITTE. There'll be no talking Not now. First I'll
have my money back.

CLAIRE Brigitte, put down the

IAN Ah, Brigitte it's a fine sight, you with a gun A good Christian woman who'd never hurt anyone. The same as all of us you are with a gun in your hand

MICHAEL Ian, let's go' We'll all talk later We'll get Brigitte's money and we'll

IAN Brigitte We'll help you get your money back. You don't want to hurt anyone with that.

BRIGITTE It's true I don't, Ian I just want my money Now both of you leave and don't come back until you have it.

IAN *(He steps toward her but stops when she cocks the gun)* That book in the wrong hands could get Michael killed, Brigitte

BRIGITTE It would take less than that book There's too many here knows too much You tried to kill Timothy There's no reason I can see why you'd not kill me or anyone here *(IAN shrugs his shoulders and begins to turn away as if he is preparing to leave, but he swings around again and grabs for the gun. He struggles with BRIGITTE and the gun fires twice BRIGITTE falls to the floor)*

MICHAEL No, Jesus Christ, no . Brigitte .. no ... Brigitte . no . I didn't want. *(MICHAEL picks her up and carries her to the sofa He holds her)*

CLAIRE. *(Puts pillows behind BRIGITTE to support her)* Brigitte! Brigitte'

KATE Oh my God, no' Brigitte

TIMOTHY. Brigitte! No...

KEITH Brigitte!

TIMOTHY No . No

KATE. Timothy, towels. I'll get a blanket.

IAN Michael, I'm sorry'

KATE *(to IAN)* Go and get a doctor' *(IAN runs out the UL door)*

MICHAEL. Get a doctor' Ian' Brigitte No I'm sorry

BRIGITTE Michael I've loved you so much You're wrong and there's no way to show you it's not worth it. It's all so simple, you know It would go away but we keep teaching the children

MICHAEL Brigitte . sit quiet you'll be alright.

BRIGITTE Claire, Michael owes us You take the money

CLAIRE Brigitte, stop this

MICHAEL We'll go, Brigitte We'll go to America. You and me and Timothy

KEITH You'll be alright, Brig

BRIGITTE Keith and Claire, you go Will you? To America ... will you...

KEITH Aye. Aye We will, Brigitte We will

BRIGITTE Michael as long as you keep worrying about County Tyrone. you'll be running It's the Earl family running again Four hundred years and . still . *(Her head falls back slightly as she goes limp)*

MICHAEL *(He shakes her as if to revive her)* Brigitte' *(He buries his head against her)* Brigitte' We'll go We'll go You and me We'll have a baby We'll go' *(He continues during the rest of the scene to cry with his head against her He rocks her as he continues promising that they will go and have a baby)* We'll go We'll go We'll have a baby, Brigitte You and me We'll go *(He continues CLAIRE turns away and leans against the doorway leading to the upstairs TIMOTHY leans against the sofa and stares blankly at the floor)*

KATE *(Stands near MICHAEL and puts her hands on his head to comfort him She looks around the room before she speaks Softly)* I knew it was here again.

CLAIRE. *(After a pause she speaks softly and haltingly)* Keith Did.. did you mean it? Would you.. leave here? Will you go with me like you said?

KEITH *(He doesn't turn to face her, he stares at BRIGITTE)* Aye, Claire. I would *(pause)* There's a few things to be done first, but we can. Someday. Someday we will.

(CLAIRE stands motionless as the light fades to a spot on her and then to a blackout)

THE END

RADIO BROADCASTS

*Note The length of the broadcasts varies from 60 to 90 seconds,
approximately They are not intended to be heard in their entirety
but the length will allow enough time for any easy scene change —
fade to blackout and lights up again The broadcast should fade in
and be the loudest at the blackout and fade out again as the next
scene opens (or the broadcast will stop when the characters turn off
the radio)*

BROADCAST — ACT I, SCENE 1
. and Prime Minister Faulkner made it very clear that it
was only a "vicious rumor" He stated further that he had
received personal assurances from Prime Minister Heath
that the suspension of Stormont was not planned Faulkner reiterated his opinion that Direct Rule would be a disaster for the people of Northern Ireland

In Andersontown today a meeting of *Women Together*
had to be cancelled because of interruptions caused by a
group of Republican women The Republican women,
led by Maire Drumm, staged a demonstration to object to
the appearance, by invitation, of Mrs Nigel Fisher. Mrs
Fisher, wife of a British Tory MP and daughter of a well-
known Ulster Unionist family, was speaking against the
IRA The demonstration by *Women Together* was peaceful
Maire Drumm, speaking in front of Central Hall, urged

the women of the Six Counties to support their menfolk. The demonstration was planned when the Belfast Speaker ran an alarming report which claimed that *Women Together* would begin handing IRA members over to the Army Claire Strain, spokeswoman for *Women Together*, said, in Cookstown today, that although the organization is against violence of any kind, it does not suggest to its members that they should turn IRA members over to the authorities Miss Strain claimed that the article was an obvious attempt by the Unionist newspaper to turn the IRA and all the Nationalists of Northern Ireland against *Women Together*

At Coalisland today the R.U.C captured six Long Kesh escapees who had been at large for several days. The prisoners were questioned by the R.U C. and the Army before they .

BROADCAST — ACT I, SCENE 2
claimed that there had not been any torture and that all statements to the contrary were false. In only the second week since the Government of Northern Ireland instituted its internment policy, 422 men have been seized and imprisoned by the Royal Ulster Constabulary. The British Government and Storment continue to deny all reports of brutality. Dublin's Irish Press reported today that Patrick Cavan, a civil rights leader from Toomebridge, was admitted to St. Stephen's Hospital after being released from Long Kesh Prison two days ago. Doctors report that Mr Cavan is suffering from severe, acute anxiety According to Mr. Cavan, he had been taken into custody by members of the British Army in Northern Ireland

and taken to a room in a building where he was forced to keep his hands above his head, or straight in front of him, for many hours while being interrogated When he let his hands fall he was struck on the abdomen until he raised them again. He was also subjected to compression of the testicles and he was allowed only two hours of sleep out of twenty-four. The interrogation was conducted by members of the Royal Ulster Constabulary and the British Army According to Matthew Donaghy, an official spokesman for the IRA, the ill treatment of prisoners at Long Kesh is mild in comparison to the horrors reported at the British Army Barracks at Holywood in County Down.

In Portadown today, sixteen schoolchildren were taken from St. Mary's Parish School to the police station in Springfield Road for questioning by the R.U.C. None were held for more than three hours, but Sister Teresa, the Mother Superior of the Sisters of Notre Dame, was kept at the station...

BROADCAST — ACT I, SCENE 3.
... and that although the parade had been banned by the local authorities, a final approval was subject to the Prime Minister.

At the Ministry of Defense today, the inquiry into the details surrounding the deaths of fourteen civil rights demonstrators killed in Derry two weeks ago continued. After lengthly questioning, the Army has had to admit that part of their report, which was published immediately after the violence, was false. Many of the statements made by soldiers at the scene were fabrications None of the men killed had been listed as persons wanted by the

authorities, as was previously claimed The Ministry of
Defence sent apologies to the relatives of the four dead
men about whom the statement had been made At least
one paratrooper has admitted that he was lying, when, in
a television interview following the shootings, he reported that he had seen one of the demonstrators shooting a
gun Lord Brockway, who was with the demonstrators in
Derry at the time of the outbreak spoke about the incident
in the House of Lords today He reported that there was
no shooting at the Army Lord Bentley labelled as pro-
paganda, a statement by the British Information Service,
which alleged that one of the fourteen men had four nail
bombs in his pocket. Frank Lagan, Chief Superintendent
of the Royal Ulster Constabulary in Derry City, claimed
that he had advised the British Army not to stop the
demonstration He thought it would be best to observe
the march so that the leaders could be identified and
prosecuted afterward for breaking the law Both the Army
Command and the Security Council ignored his advice
on the demonstration and stationed soldiers at each in-
tersection

BROADCAST — ACT II, SCENE 1
(Optional — can be used at the end of the break between acts)
there was only one injury in the clash that followed Mr
Frank Cregagh of Ballygomartin Road was taken to the
Crumlin Road Hospital in Cliftonville where he was
treated for facial cuts The Executive Committee of the
Anti-Partition League sent an official letter of protest to
Prime Minister Faulkner today, demanding to know why
he had granted permission to the Orange Lodges of Kil-

keel and Cranfield to march through the Catholic area
around Long Stone Road Mr Faulkner claimed that this
was not a case of "coat-trailing" "It was not the intention
of the Orangemen," he said, "to give offence to anyone,
but they would not yield one iota of their freedom to
march where they pleased, nor would they tolerate
threats of interference with their processions " The Anti-
Partition League reminded Faulkner that he had refused
permission to the city of Derry for the Nationalist St Patrick's Day Parade on the grounds that such a procession
would require unreasonable efforts on the part of the
police force Yet Stormont, the league went on to say, had
provided 600 armed police, complete with commando
units, to force a passageway for the Orange march
through the nearly exclusive Nationalist/Catholic area of
Long Stone Road Wireless equipment and tear gas were
issued to the police who backed up the Orange marchers.
The Royal Ulster Constabulary was described by those
present as "jackbooted like the Storm Troopers of Hitler's
Germany " Mr. Faulkner would not comment on the use
of police at the Orange march nor on his refusal to grant a
permit for the Nationalist parade in Derry In his summa-
tion he claimed that in all cases he followed the laws of the
Unionist Government in Northern Ireland Albert Monaghan, official spokesman of the League, commented on
Faulkner's actions in a speech in Dungiven this evening.
"The only law known in Northern Ireland," he said, "is
the law that the Orange Lodges are pleased to approve "
Monaghan condemned the Orange march in South
Down as an attempt to stir up trouble. He compared the
situation to a group of Nationalists marching to Mass via

Shankhill Road "One can imagine the outcry," he said

BROADCAST — ACT II, SCENE 2
in a speech given in Parliament last Thursday

Secretary of State, William Whitelaw, was speaking in defence of recent British actions in Northern Ireland He stated again Parliament's determination to afford all citizens of Northern Ireland the fullest protection of the law in combatting the IRA terrorist campaign and the activities of Protestant extremists These are his words

(British speaker) "There can be no change in the constitutional position of Northern Ireland as part of the United Kingdom unless by the will of the majority Equally, of course, if the majority of the people in Northern Ireland were to opt for a United Ireland, no British Government would stand in the way. But, here I must say something to all those who want a United Ireland and who think they can get it by violence and by force, who think they can somehow bomb the majority of the Protestant community into a United Ireland I say to them that they cannot, that they will not and that there is no possible chance of their doing it. I say to them that the longer they go on with the violence, the further away will be the objective they seek to promote "

(back to Irish speaker) In Belfast today an unnamed IRA member was shot in his car as he attempted a getaway from the area of Shankhill Road where a bomb had just exploded The driver lost control of the car and slammed into another car on the roadside. Three children were crushed to death in the accident. Their identities have not been determined

An early morning fire in Derry took the lives of three women The fire occured in the Parish House of the Little Flower Church in Brigend Road No causes were immediately

BROADCAST — ACT II, SCENE 3

in a report issued by Sir Edmund Compton and by Lord Palmer All reports of torture or any inhuman methods of interrogation will be thoroughly checked according to an official in Lord Palmer's service The Commission agreed that several persons in Northern Ireland were arrested on the grounds that they were politically active and the Stormont Government feared they would be potential organizers of protests against the internment policy This "politically active" group includes Socialists, Communists, members of the People's Democracy, and leaders of the Northern Ireland Civil Rights Association

In Derry today the Scotland Yard Special Detective Force began an investigation into the death of Samuel Devenney of Bogside His family claims that several R.U C policemen, clad in helmets, visors, heavily-armoured clothing, carrying shields, pistols and long riot-batons, invaded their home in Bogside Witnesses claimed that Devenney himself, his wife and their young children were badly beaten Mr Devenney, already in poor health, died shortly thereafter. The Special Detective Force said today that their investigation was already at a standstill because they have encountered a "wall of silence" from the police in Derry Not one member of the R U C would say who had been in the squad that attacked Devenney's house Sir Arthur Young, Inspector-General of the R. U C., reported today in Belfast that he was considering resigning his post in light of the lack of cooperation given to Scotland Yard in their investigation.

"What is good for Northern Ireland is good for the Unionist Party." So said Prime Minister Faulkner in an address to the East Down Unionists in Strangford. It was the first time the Prime Minister has admitted to any need for reform in the six counties of...

PLAYWRIGHT'S NOTE

In the history of Ireland, *the flight of the earls* is an event of great importance In 1607 the Earls of Tyrone and Tyr-connell fled Ireland to escape British oppression They hoped to gather an army on the continent which would help them push the English out of Ireland forever The departure of the Earls made it easier for the British to establish a Protestant settlement in Northern Ireland — over three hundred and fifty years ago Still, the un-resolved England/Ireland dispute is part of daily life in the six counties of Northern Ireland

In 1971, the time in which this play is set, the British government, seeing that the Protestant government of Brian Faulkner in Northern Ireland was unable to stop repeated outbreaks of terrorism, instituted a policy of *internment* by which many hundreds of men were rounded up and imprisoned without charges The treatment of the men so interned was brutal Subsequent investigations by Amnesty International and by the British government itself, revealed that the British Army had used torture on many of the internees It was Northern Ireland's most violent outbreak of the last thirty years

PROPERTIES

The set should include whatever would be appropriate for the living room/dining room of the Earl home (see set description) The items which are specifically used by the characters in the play include.

THROUGHOUT THE PLAY
  On the breakfront.
    Whiskey bottles
    Glasses
    China (plates, cups, saucers)
    Telephone

ACT I

  Scene 1
    Pocket radio — Timothy
    Net shopping bag — Kate
    Dress box — Kate

  Scene 2
    Tablecloth (taken from the breakfront) — Kate
    Small money box (taken from the breakfront) — Kate
    Money (British pound notes) — Brigitte
    Small pocket radio w/earplug (giftwrapped) — Brigitte

  Scene 3
    Handgun — Keith

ACT II

Scene 1
Handwritten letter — Brigitte
Handgun — Kate
Car keys — Claire

Scene 3
Bandage (for Keith's leg)
Ledger book — Brigitte
Desk key — Brigitte
Dish cloth — Timothy
Blanket — Kate

COSTUMES

All the characters, except Claire, should be dressed very simply as would be appropriate for a farm/garage in the Irish countryside Claire would be a little more fashionable or "tailored" Ian and Michael wear grease-stained overalls over their regular clothing, which they take off and hang on the coatrack when they are finished working or are leaving the farm Each character would wear, or have hanging on the coatrack, a light jacket or coat (very plain) Although the play takes place in September, the evening would be very cool

SPECIFIC ITEMS
   Overalls — Michael and Ian
   Workboots — Michael and Ian
   New blue dress — Kate
   Hat — Kate
   House shoes — Kate
   Wristwatch (leather strap) — Michael
   Handbag — Claire
   Attaché case — Claire
   Apron — Kate
   Cap — Keith
   Boots — Keith
   Black pullover sweater — Michael

GENERAL ITEMS (all characters)
   Coats or jackets

THE SCENE
Theresa Rebeck

Little Theatre / Drama / 2m, 2f / Interior Unit Set
A young social climber leads an actor into an extra-marital
affair, from which he then creates a full-on downward spiral
into alcoholism and bummery. His wife runs off with his best
friend, his girlfriend leaves, and he's left with… nothing.

"Ms. Rebeck's dark-hued morality tale contains enough fresh
insights into the cultural landscape to freshen what is essen-
tially a classic boy-meets-bad-girl story."
- *New York Times*

"Rebeck's wickedly scathing observations about the sort of
self-obsessed New Yorkers who pursue their own interests at
the cost of their morality and loyalty."
- *New York Post*

"The Scene is utterly delightful in its comedic performances,
and its slowly unraveling plot is thought-provoking and gut-
wrenching."
- *Show Business Weekly*

THREE MUSKETEERS
Ken Ludwig

All Groups / Adventure / 8m, 4f (doubling) / Unit sets

This adaptation is based on the timeless swashbuckler by Alexandre Dumas, a tale of heroism, treachery, close escapes and above all, honor. The story, set in 1625, begins with d'Artagnan who sets off for Paris in search of adventure. Along with d'Artagnan goes Sabine, his sister, the quintessential tomboy. Sent with d'Artagnan to attend a convent school in Paris, she poses as a young man – d'Artagnan's servant – and quickly becomes entangled in her brother's adventures. Soon after reaching Paris, d'Artagnan encounters the greatest heroes of the day, Athos, Porthos and Aramis, the famous musketeers; d'Artagnan joins forces with his heroes to defend the honor of the Queen of France. In so doing, he finds himself in opposition to the most dangerous man in Europe, Cardinal Richelieu. Even more deadly is the infamous Countess de Winter, known as Milady, who will stop at nothing to revenge herself on d'Artagnan – and Sabine – for their meddlesome behavior. Little does Milady know that the young girl she scorns, Sabine, will ultimately save the day.

SAMUEL FRENCH STAFF

Nate Collins
President

Ken Dingledine
Director of Operations,
Vice President

Bruce Lazarus
Executive Director

Rita Maté
Director of Finance

ACCOUNTING

Lori Thimsen | Director of Licensing Compliance
Mehal Kumar | Senior Accounting Associate
Josephine Messina | Accounts Payable
Helena Mezzina | Royalty Administration
Joe Garner | Royalty Administration
Jessica Zheng | Accounts Receivable
Andy Lian | Accounts Receivable
Joe Qiu | Accounts Receivable
Charlie Sou | Accounting Associate
Joann Mannello | Orders Administrator

BUSINESS AFFAIRS

Sasna Marzani | Director of Business Affairs
Kathryn McCumber | Business Administrator

CUSTOMER SERVICE AND LICENSING

Brad Lohrenz | Director of Licensing Development
Ellie Davis | Licensing Service Manager
Fred Schnitzer | Business Development Manager
Melody Fernandez | Amateur Licensing Supervisor
Laura Lindson | Professional Licensing Supervisor
John Tracey | Professional Licensing Associate
Kim Rogers | Amateur Licensing Associate
Matthew Akers | Amateur Licensing Associate
Ly Clark | Amateur Licensing Associate
Alicia Grey | Amateur Licensing Associate
Ashley Byrne | Amateur Licensing Associate
Mike Glickman | Amateur Licensing Associate
Chris Lonstrup | Amateur Licensing Associate
Jez Zuniga | Amateur Licensing Associate
Glenn Halcomb | Amateur Licensing Associate
Derek Hassler | Amateur Licensing Associate
Jennifer Carter | Amateur Licensing Associate

EDITORIAL AND PUBLICATIONS

Amy Rose Marsh | Literary Manager
Ben Coleman | Editorial Associate
Gene Sweeney | Graphic Designer
David Geer | Publications Supervisor
Charlyn Brea | Publications Associate
Tyler Mullen | Publications Associate

MARKETING

Abbie Van Nostrand | Director of Marketing
Alison Sundstrom | Marketing Associate

OPERATIONS

Joe Ferreira | Product Development Manager
Casey McLain | Operations Supervisor
Danielle Heckman | Office Coordinator, Reception

SAMUEL FRENCH BOOKSHOP (LOS ANGELES)

Joyce Mehess | Bookstore Manager
Cory DeLair | Bookstore Buyer
Jennifer Palumbo | Customer Service Associate
Sonya Wallace | Bookstore Associate
Tim Coultas | Bookstore Associate
Monté Patterson | Bookstore Associate
Robin Hushbeck | Bookstore Associate
Alfred Contreras | Shipping & Receiving

LONDON OFFICE

Felicity Barks | Submissions Associate
Steve Blacker | Bookshop Associate
David Bray | Customer Services Associate
Zena Choi | Professional Licensing Associate
Robert Cooke | Assistant Buyer
Stephanie Dawson | Amateur Licensing Associate
Simon Ellison | Retail Sales Manager
Jason Felix | Royalty Administration
Susan Griffiths | Amateur Licensing Associate
Robert Hamilton | Amateur Licensing Associate
Lucy Hume | Publications Associate
Nasir Khan | Management Accountant
Simon Magniti | Royalty Administration
Louise Mappley | Amateur Licensing Associate
James Nicolau | Despatch Associate
Martin Phillips | Librarian
Zubayed Rahman | Despatch Associate
Steve sanderson | Royalty Administration Supervisor
Roger Sheppard | I.T. Manager
Geoffrey Skinner | Company Accountant
Peter Smith | Amateur Licensing Associate
Garry Spratley | Customer Service Manager
David Webster | UK Operations Director

SAMUELFRENCH.COM
SAMUELFRENCH-LONDON.CO.UK

GET THE NAME OF YOUR CAST AND CREW IN PRINT WITH SPECIAL EDITIONS!

Special Editions are a unique, fun way to commemorate your production and RAISE MONEY.

The Samuel French Special Edition is a customized script personalized to *your* production. Your cast and crew list, photos from your production and special thanks will all appear in a Samuel French Acting Edition alongside the original text of the play.

These Special Editions are powerful fundraising tools that can be sold in your lobby or throughout your community in advance.

These books have autograph pages that make them perfect for year book memories, or gifts for relatives unable to attend the show. Family and friends will cherish this one of a kind souvenier.

Everyone will want a copy of these beautiful, personalized scripts!

ORDER YOUR COPIES TODAY!
E-MAIL SPECIALEDITIONS@SAMUELFRENCH.COM
OR CALL US AT 1-866-598-8449!